WILD FLORA
OF THE
NORTHEAST

Mountain laurel (*Kalmialatofolia*)

WILD FLORA of the

Anita and Spider Barbour

NORTHEAST

 THE OVERLOOK PRESS   WOODSTOCK, NEW YORK

View of Catskill Mountains from Sickler Road,
Woodstock, New York

First Published in 1991 by
The Overlook Press
Lewis Hollow Road
Woodstock, New York 12498

Library of Congress Cataloging-in-Publication Data

Barbour, Spider.
      Wild flora of the Northeast / Spider & Anita Babour.
            p.   cm.
      Includes index.
      1. Botany—Northeastern States.   2. Plant communities—
Northeastern States.   3. Botany—Northeastern States—Pictorial
works.   I. Barbour, Anita. II. Title.

QK117.B27 1989
582.0974—dc19   88-22422
ISBN 0-87951-344-6   CIP

Designed by Abigail Sturges
Printed in Hong Kong by South China Printing Company (1988) Limited

CONTENTS

Dogbane (*Apocynum*) pod in Krumville, New York

INTRODUCTION

COMPETITION is a natural process, part of the behavior of most wild organisms, and common in our own species. Competitiveness was seen by post-Darwinists as the major dynamic in evolution, as expressed in the doctrine of "survival of the fittest." In more recent years, many biologists have stressed as equally important the development of co-operative relationships in nature in which organisms "trade services" without injuring each other.

I can think of this book in terms of either competition or cooperation. It is a nature book with photographs, and an awful lot of those have been published over the last seventy-five years or so. In the last two decades especially, public interest in nature and the environment has burgeoned, and with it, all sorts of published materials on the subject. So this book has competition, but I'd rather emphasize the co-operative. No matter how many nature books with beautiful photos are published, can we really have enough of these? If such books help in any way to slow down the alarming rate of environmental destruction wrought by those among us who are not swayed by beautiful photographs and pleading poetics, if these books can rouse to action those with a sympathy for the beauty and value of pristine nature, then the more the better.

Biologists are different from nature-lovers (though obviously they love nature) in being better educated in the field. Of course, there is in reality, a gradation of levels of knowledge, similar to what biologists call a cline. But if two extremes are assumed—that of the highly-trained scientist and that of the nature-lover exposed only to the average input popular culture provides—then we see a difference. The professional ecologist sees a forest or a bog or a meadow, but also sees a system, an integrated, evolved, interdependent community of organisms, of species. The biologist sees the forest for the trees and the trees for the forest. The biologist looks, and knows what species are there, and may then predict with accuracy what bedrock lies beneath the soil and how deeply, whether the soil is well-drained, tends to sog, how old is the present growth, and many other facts which probably would never even occur as questions in the mind of a less-educated observer.

Yet anyone with curiosity can look at a thing and the thing will almost ask questions itself. And usually, anyone with some intelligence can find a way to the answer. The great Swiss naturalist Louis Agassiz wondered why huge boulders from distant bedrock formations were strewn about the forests and pastures of southern Europe. He correctly concluded they were carried there by ice during a glacial age long ago. But he also found that in places where glaciers still sometimes advanced across a mile or so of mountain valley and then retreated, the common shepherds knew well the origin of giant rocks in the fields. Scientific knowledge is not the exclusive domain of academics.

Scientists are those who professionally seek answers to the mysteries of the universe, and making this their lives, they grow in knowledge and erudition far beyond the limits of what entomologist Frank Lutz called "the laity." In our present culture there is, to borrow a term of recent political vintage, a "trickle down" from the loftiest heights of science to the people on the street (or more accurately, the people at home watching TV). Some make careers of translating esoteric modern science into popular language, because there is a need in a democratic country for the populace to be sufficiently informed so as to make political decisions from a vantage point of adequate knowledge. Also, people are interested in science, people want to know how the world works.

It seems to me, however, that science, including biology, has become something of a spectator sport recently, with most of people's input coming from television nature documentaries, from books and magazines, and from news reports about environmental conflicts and disasters. The effect of this, though I'm not sure, may be to have distanced many people from the immediacy of nature in their lives. The exotic has become commonplace, now that the average American family can take a video vacation to the sands of the Namib, the rain forests of Ceylon, the frozen wastes of the Antarctic or the deepest depths of the Pacific. We leaf through pages of beautiful photographs of beautiful living things more often than we go forth to find the real thing. We contribute to conservation organizations to save whales, rain forests, rhinos and pine barrens, but don't visit the places we help to preserve. Others discover such places or recognize that habitats and organisms are in need of saving and then seek to convince the rest of us to do what we can. This is certainly good, but I believe people need more of a direct experience.

I realize not everyone can afford to safari to Kenya, the Galapagos or Madagascar. I couldn't afford it either. But the exotic is where you find it. We've been subtly taught that what's amazing, beautiful and worth seeing is far from home. But is it? One of the most unusual nature documentaries presented in the past few years was one about Point Pelee in Ontario, a peninsula that juts out into Lake Ontario. It's a homey place, populated by many of the same plants and animals we find near our home in the Hudson Valley. I was a bit surprised to find myself getting more excited about seeing tulip trees and hognose snakes on TV than I get seeing pottos and acacias. There's something stimulating about seeing the familiar presented as entertainment. It was very much like watching a friend of ours as a guest on the Joan Rivers show. "Wow! There's Dan! He's really good! Hey!" Well, the cottonwoods and bluebirds of Ontario's Point Pelee were good, too.

Things are even better "in person." I have a much better time walking in my back yard and finding a slimy salamander or a trout lily than I do watching cheetahs run down gazelles on "Wild Kingdom" reruns. It's this addiction to the real natural world, the closest patch of wild forest or old field to home, that I wish to promote. And I'd like to encourage a thirst for knowledge and an ability to see readily the questions nature asks, the queries posed by the lean of a weathered pine, the proliferation of spring flowers in a mountain hollow, the stunted trees on a high ridge above a river, the presence of cacti on the rocky ground behind an urban shopping center, the identity of a flowering vine growing from the pebbled bed of a mountain stream.

The setting for this book is the most populated region of the United States, the Northeast. This region has a rich and venerable tradition of naturalists and nature writers, ecological research and the conservation of wild habitats. It has also been the arena of conflict in many battles between those whose purposes demanded the destruction of natural habitats and those who fought to preserve them. The war between these forces continues, revealing a breach of knowledge and attitude far more extreme than that between professional scientist and weekend nature buff. At a hearing on a development proposed for a section of the Pine Bush, a rare plant community in Albany, New York, the developer was overheard to say during an intermission, "Butterflies? Butterflies? They want to stop me because of butterflies??" Ironically, but typically, the people whose attitudes need most to be changed are those least likely to expose themselves to the information that might convince them.

I would be too optimistic to hope a developer such as the one so perplexed by ecologists' defense of butterflies might pick up this book and come away from it with a new appreciation of the natural resources of his home region, and be resolved to examine more carefully the places he wants to build malls and condominiums. There are places where even the most militant conservationist would concede that it's all right to build homes or factories or shopping centers. But some places are too precious to destroy; there are too few examples of such places or perhaps this is the last place of its kind. Many valuable natural sites have been destroyed because no one was there to tell people how rare a thing they were losing. Someday there may be no place left to build, but until then, we must preserve the most uncommon environments and try to keep even the common ones from becoming scarce.

To do this we need two things—a passion for the natural world around us and a restless inquisitiveness that urges us to find out about the world. People need the conviction that home is where the heart is, that the immediate everyday neighborhood is full of wonders, as it truly is. The things we take for granted or take little notice of, the patch of weeds by the mailbox, the hollow pine tree on the back hill, the strange stretch of little "Christmas trees" growing on white rocks along the highway, all

Horse nettle (*Solanum carolinense*) berries

Red cedar (*Juniperus virginianum*) berries

these things have special, wonderful stories to impart. All these stories add up to a complex saga of life in a most fascinating corner of the planet.

What this book is, in light of what's been written so far, is a sampler and primer for understanding the natural communities of the Northeast, and more than that, a gallery for the photographs of some of the region's most beautiful natural objects. Its intent is not so much to impart an education or engage in a comprehensive and exhaustive survey of the life of the region, but rather to engage the reader's imagination in the discovery that the most familiar things are just as wonderful as things presented as exotic (and therefore of more interest) than things close to home. All things are interesting given enough knowledge about them to make them so. It's a cliche among scientists that the more one knows the more one realizes there is still to be known. So this book couldn't tell you everything there is to know about the Northeast's natural communities even if I had spent sixty years on it instead of six.

It is important that knowledge, what we are told is true, can be experienced, can be seen, felt, heard and proved to be true by real experience. Throughout this book I have tried to connect the more crucial scientific facts about the Northeast's natural history to what a person can witness by going out into the woods or fields or swamps and watching, listening and thinking. We begin with an overview of the recent history of the Northeast, from the time it was covered by a huge sheet of glacial ice that had crept down from the polar regions, to the present day, and a cursory survey of the most important plant communities.

The remainder of the book is a seasonal tour of Northeast plant communities, beginning with the first greening and blooming of early spring and continuing through the growing season to the senescence of autumn and the dormancy of winter.

A professor of mine said he preferred six seasons rather than four, adding a "pre-vernal" season (the thaw that leads to "vernal" or true spring) and a pre-autumnal "serotinal" season to emphasize the heightened vegetative and insect activity of late summer/early fall. This system has its merits, as it follows more closely the patterns in nature than the celestial seasons. I've made use of both systems, since one is more accurate and the other more familiar. Actually, natural cycles are more or less gradual, and seasonal transitions cannot be pinned down to exact dates. With this in mind, I have emphasized the succession of natural processes rather than try to establish a date chronology.

The photographs and drawings by Anita, my wife and constant companion on nature excursions, are more momentous than anything I could write about the things they portray and celebrate. In her photographs, Anita has taken plants and mushrooms beyond the appearance they present to us in reality, creating what seem to be, at their best, paintings on film. Such abstracted images are not diagnostic, but simply beautiful. They are always a surprise to me, because I can never tell while looking at the thing being photographed, what the picture will be like. There's always something new, something unseen before—a leaf becomes a castle, a twig a knight on horseback, a mushroom a duck's head. These fanciful outcomes are occasional and specific; what's new in one of these photographs is more often the entire world revealed there. A new perspective is created where the common objects of the woods and fields become larger than life, or the viewer is scaled down to the dimensions of mosses and tiny mushrooms growing from a leaf stem.

After seeing Anita's photographs I return to nature with a new set of senses, closer to those of the tiny creatures who live among dead leaves and high grasses, those that fly from flower to flower or scale the walls of limestone escarpments or prowl the deep shade of hemlock-roofed ravines.

The device has not yet been invented that allows people to see through other species' eyes, but realizing that other eyes exist and see things differently from the way we do—that's the beginning of a naturalist's enlightenment. I hope these words and pictures will spark that process in many and keep it going in those who've already taken the first step.

THE NORTHEAST
AS A BIOREGION

To describe the circumference of the Northeast is not as simple as it might appear. Taking some central point as the hub of the nation (St. Louis, for example) we could mark lines in the four major directions, carving the country into quarters. Would the northeast quarter of this scheme be The Northeast, as most Americans conceive of it? No, since it includes the states known as the Midwest—Illinois, Indiana and Ohio, as well as Kentucky, Tennessee and the Virginias, considered southern states. Many subtle and unconscious notions are brought to play in trying to define a region of the country, among them social considerations such as regional accents, geographical boundaries and the sense of a community or region held by its natives and by residents of neighboring regions. For these reasons there are many ideas as to what constitutes the Northeast or any other region of the country.

Since this book is about flora—the many kinds of plants which grow in the region—I will try to define the Northeast in terms of regionally distinct plant communities. Botanists and ecologists have divided the country into sections according to several different schemes. Victor E. Shelford, in *The Ecology of North America* (1978, University of Illinois Press, Urbana) describes "The Temperate Deciduous Forest Biome," which includes New England, New York, Pennsylvania, Ohio, Kentucky, Tennessee, Indiana, Illinois, Missouri, Wisconsin and Minnesota as well as the Maritimes, southern Ontario and Southern Quebec in Canada; Kulik et al., in *The Audubon Field Guide to the Natural Places of the Northeast* (1984, The Hilltown Press, Inc. and Pantheon Press, New York) shows the Northeast as New York State and the New England states. The latter is a guide to nature preserves in the region and is not concerned with botanical descriptions or ecological boundaries. New York and New England are the core of the Northeast covered by the book you are reading, but the descriptions of plant communities apply fairly well to Shelford's larger temperate forest biome.

Ten to twelve thousand years ago, ice sheets still covered nearly all of New York and New England. The limit of glacial influence is a valid southern boundary for the Northeast. Westward, the boundary must be more arbitrary. The Great Lakes, glacially gouged basins that later filled

Dame's rocket (*Hesperus matronalis*)

Previous pages: Phoenicia evening

with water, greatly influenced the botanical character of the lands around them, and so may be regarded as a valid western boundary. Eastward, the Atlantic Ocean is the logical boundary. Southeastern Canada is botanically similar to the United States immediately across the border, so the material in this book applies to southern Ontario and Quebec.

Plant Communities

The term "plant community" may be an unfamiliar one to some. First, it denotes an assemblage of plant species growing in the same geographic location, but more than that, a group of plants characteristic of a particular geography and tending to assemble as a repetitious species array. Botanists recognize plants in such associations, since the plants behave in an associative manner. This is because the prevailing conditions in a given area (such an area may be of almost any size, from less than an acre to millions of square miles), if uniform, will tend to support best those plants best adapted to those environmental conditions. Thus, a plant community is a group of plants with very similar ecologies of climate, moisture and soil. They may, indeed they must, differ considerably in other aspects of their respective ecologies—size, time of bloom, type of pollinator, seed form and means of dispersal (here I'm referring just to angiosperms: flowering plants), so they are not in direct competition with one another. Most plant communities contain a great variety of plants in a well-segregated size hierarchy—trees, shrubs, herbs, grasses, mosses and lichens. There is often considerable diversity within each of these size groups.

The predominant plant communities in the Northeast are forests, communities dominated by trees. Given the Northeast's moist climate and well-developed soils, non-forest communities tend to be displaced by forests over time. Only where soil, moisture or weather conditions are locally extraordinary, do we find exceptions to this rule. Such exceptional environments include high mountains, shores, bare rock exposures where soil can't easily accumulate, and certain kinds of soil such as deep sands

Shadbush (*Amelanchier laevis*)

Amanita vaginata mushroom

Pluteus petasatus mushroom

and clays in which young trees usually die before their roots grow deep enough to reach water.

The forests of the Northeast are sometimes divided into those dominated by conifers ("evergreens" such as pines, spruces and firs) and those dominated by hardwoods or deciduous trees (also called "broadleaved trees" to distinguish them from those with needles). Within these two broad divisions, finer distinctions can be made among forest types. To confuse matters, the real world is filled with mixtures of all kinds of trees, hardwoods and evergreens, but certain forest communities are little varying and easily distinguished from others. More interestingly, the underlying soil and moisture conditions of a place, and its prevailing weather and climate, can be read from the plants which grow there.

Glacial Effects

The various forest systems of the region follow a geographic scheme related to climate and to historic events. The glacial advances and retreats of the Pleistocene epoch are a major historic influence on Northeast plant communities. More recently, human alteration of the environment has caused significant changes in these communities.

The immense, all-pervasive Laurentide ice sheet, a glacial Gargantua over a mile thick, overran virtually all of New England and New York north of northern Long Island. The terminal moraine, a tremendous ridge of debris dropped by the ice sheet at its southern limit, runs the length of Long Island, showing it to have been about half covered by ice.

All vegetation was swept away southward or ground to rubble beneath the pressure of countless tons of ice, which under such weight becomes slowly fluid, inexorably oozing across the land until it melts away in a warmer climate south of its frigid place of origin. Our present floral landscape has arisen only in the ten or twelve thousand years since the glaciers began retreating northward. During the decline of the glaciers, plants settled in from areas outside those covered by ice. Because the previous advance of the ice had been slow, plant communities were not

Wild oats/sessile bellwort
(*Uvularia sessilifolia*)

wiped out, though individual plants certainly were. The glaciers pushed zones of vegetation (such as those described as "hardiness zones" in garden catalogs) southward and probably compressed them into narrower bands than they occupy today. At the time of maximum glaciation, arctic tundra vegetation occupied northern Pennsylvania and southwestern New York State. South of this zone was a conifer forest like that found today in most of southern Canada and the mountains of New York and New England. Georgia was probably largely covered by northern hardwood forest.

Glaciers covered most of Europe at the same time they occupied North America. In Europe, the ice extinguished many species of plants by pressing southward to the Alps. The North American flora, encountering no mountain barriers to the south, survived the ice age apparently with little or no species loss. This will have bearing on the discussion of native fungi later in this book.

It is tempting to imagine the post-glacial landscape as a barren jumble of rocks and rubble, cut by quick brown streams of glacial meltwaters, but this model is probably wrong. More likely, the retreat of the ice was so slow that plants continually pressed their advantage, almost immediately taking over any land given up by the ice mass. On modern glaciers, spruce trees often grow in the soil rubble of moraines or even ride upon the glaciers where there is sufficient soil for a roothold.

Yet it is clear that plants from distant parts of the continent found passage many hundreds of miles from their native haunts by virtue of the glacier's clean sweep. The northeast flora contains several plant species found also in the western mountains, the great plains and upper midwest wetlands. Also present are plants more comfortable in an arctic climate. These have been left stranded far from their northern counterparts on the highest mountains of New York and New England. Other plants found only in the high mountains are not typical arctic plants, but true alpines, plants which are adapted not merely to cold and a short growing season, but to the particular stresses of high peaks and ridges, the high winds, sudden frosts and thin air of mountains.

Still other elements of the Northeast flora arrived from the south—

Walking fern (*Camptosorus rhizophyllus*)

21

elements of the unglaciated coastal plain, piedmont and southern Appalachian floras. Notable among these plants are those of the "pine barrens" communities found on glacial lake sands and dry, thin-soiled uplands of some river valleys. Other southern plants are present as elements of forests and other kinds of communities (wetlands, especially), but do not form a community type as distinct as the pine barrens flora.

The post-glacial development of vegetation in the region has been studied extensively, but there is disagreement among botanists as to what the evidence indicates. Pollen samples from bogs (which preserve in their acid soils identifiable pollen grains from thousands of years back) suggest warming and cooling trends and wet and dry stages over the past 10,000 years, but samples from different locations tell different stories. There is still more research to be done before an accurate picture of post-glacial vegetational change begins to emerge.

The Human Element

The influence of European settlement in the Northeast is much easier to document. Agriculture and logging were the first large-scale changes effected on the plant communities of the Northeast by human settlers. Even the native Americans practiced limited slash-and-burn farming and such techniques as burning ridge forests to increase blueberry and acorn crops. These acts simulate the effects of natural events such as lightning fires and damage inflicted by severe windstorms. But the land-use practices of Europeans were much more devastating, and have increased in scope and intensity with advancing technology and expanding population. More recently, however, with the decline in farming, much of the land once used as fields and pastures has reverted to forest. To some degree, efforts to preserve important wild lands have staved off the increasing threat of damage or destruction to many plant communities, especially the rarer ones.

An important effect of early European settlement in the New World was the introduction of many European plant species into the Northeast. Sawkill Creek

Most of these are herbs, which in botany means non-woody plants other than grasses and their near relatives and non-flowering plants such as mosses and lichens. When we speak of herbs we do not necessarily refer to plants used as spices or flavorings. Most herbs are flowering plants, so "herb" and "wildflower" are roughly equivalent in this context.

The alien plants of the Northeast include many crop plants, garden flowers which have escaped to the wild, and those accidental introductions of seeds carried on cargoes from Europe, or in some cases, Asia or other lands. In addition to these exotic intruders, some plants from the western United States have come east by one means or another and have become part of this weedy component of the Northeast flora.

For the most part these weeds compete poorly with native plants, but when the environment is disturbed—when land is cleared and plowed or the soil scraped, dug up or turned over—the alien plants gain a competitive edge and soon occupy the disturbed ground largely to the exclusion of native species.

The Northeast flora today is a rich mix of native and alien species distributed in a great diversity of communities and habitats, the variety of which is enhanced by the variety of the region's landforms, its many large and small waters—the ocean, lakes, streams, ponds and wetlands—and the north-south range of climatic extremes. The remainder of this section is a brief review of the most important plant communities of the region.

FORESTS

Northern Conifers

On a north-south, cold-warm gradient, the forests of the Northeast are conveniently divided into three major systems. Farthest north is the Canadian conifer forest, a community of cool, moist conditions dominated by evergreen trees, typically red spruce and balsam fir, and to a lesser degree, black and white spruces and tamarack in wooded wetlands. Jack pine replaces the more southern pitch pine on the driest soils. Deciduous trees occur in a secondary role: yellow and paper birches,

Half-free morel (*Morchella semilibera*)

quaking and bigtooth aspens, black cherry, pin cherry and red maple are the most common of these.

Shrubs include striped and mountain maples, hobblebush, chokeberry, blueberry, two plants named mountain holly (one is a holly; one isn't!), mountain ash, and American yew. Many of our ferns have a northern affinity, and in northern forests there will be found sunny glades blanketed by hay-scented fern and mountain woodfern, typically where a large tree has fallen and left a sunny opening in the dark woodland. Wildflowers of the Canadian forest include corn lily, goldthread, mountain wood sorrel, twisted stalk, painted trillium, twinflower, and Canada and round-leaved violets. In special habitats within this zone, wild orchids of several species grace the summer woods. These are especially fond of wetlands such as bogs and fens, but some are found in the forest.

This is the forest of the Canadian shield, of most of Ontario and Quebec, but it dominates only the coldest parts of the American Northeast, the Adirondacks of New York State, most of northern New England (the northern third of Vermont and New Hampshire and most of Maine except for the coastal lowlands), and the higher mountains of the southern part of the region. Lowland examples of this forest differ from those in mountains. Trees in the lowlands grow tall and are not very weather-stressed; those in mountains are constantly buffeted by high winds and often grow into squat and twisted forms, typically devoid of branches on the side facing the open wind.

Mountain conifer forests are variable in character, since they are continually being devastated and renewed. Even from one mountain peak to the next the forest may be entirely dissimilar. One may be old with scattered, immense firs and birches, between which grow thickets of shrubs and ferns. The next may be covered with an impenetrable growth of small spruce and fir saplings, all of nearly the same size and age, the last old trees having recently been destroyed by storm or the ravages of an insect infestation.

Lowland forests are more stable and give the feeling of cathedral-like solemnity. Here the trees rise tall, straight and stately, and little vegetation impedes the progress of the walker on the forest floor. Only where a

Lichen (*Cladina*) and moss (*Polytrichum*)

25

woodland monarch has fallen and opened the canopy to allow the sun to reach the ground in abundance do shrubs and ferns fill the space to knee level or higher. Mixed among these will be found young trees jostling each other for the eventual replacement of the fallen giant.

Northern Hardwoods

The vast center of the Northeast is held by a mixed conifer/hardwood forest traditionally called "transitional" by forest experts who consider it a gradation zone between the southern Appalachian hardwood forest and the Canadian conifer forest. This characterization is questionable; the species mix is that of the trees best adapted to the climate of the region where they grow, and the area of their occupation is too large for their community to be considered any more "transitional" than those to the north and south.

Sugar maple and American beech are the dominant hardwoods of this forest community, which I prefer to call the northern hardwood forest. White pine and hemlock are the most common coniferous trees. Many other trees occur with these dominant species, including all the hardwoods mentioned as typical of the Canadian conifer forest, plus red oak, basswood, butternut, hop hornbeam, American hornbeam, shagbark hickory and black birch. Shrubs include witch hazel, striped maple, black holly in wet soils and mountain laurel in dry, acid soils. The herbaceous community is spectacular and is treated in detail in Part Two: Spring, since it is at that season, just before the leaves appear on the trees, that nearly all the flowering herbs of the northern hardwood forest burst into bloom.

Valley Hardwoods

In the southern part of the region, the northern hardwoods begin to intermix with the Atlantic Coastal Plain/Piedmont and southern Appalachian forests, and this mix could be called a transitional system. The northern hardwoods are enriched by the most northward ranging species

Lopseed (*Phryma leptostachya*)

Virginia creeper (*Parthenocissus quinquefolia*)

of the southern forest. Prominent among these are tuliptree, tupelo, cucumber tree, pawpaw, sweetgum, a variety of oaks and hickories, and sassafras. This southern forest tends to be less rich in wildflowers than the more northern hardwood forests of the region, but in all areas the places where wildflowers are most abundant are scattered about between stretches of forest with few or no herbaceous elements. The reasons for this inconsistency will be explored in the next section.

Within all three major forest systems are found many forest communities with what might be termed "local character." This is especially true of the southern mixed forest, which is hereby dubbed valley hardwood forest, after botanist Michael Kudish's terminology (Hudson Valley Forest). In the Northeast, forests with southern elements are restricted to major river valleys, the Atlantic coast and the Ontario Lake Plain. These are the warmest parts of the region and have the longest growing seasons.

Floodplains

Floodplain forests grow on the riverine sediments brought by major floods. At least once a year these forests are under water for several days or weeks. Trees of floodplains include sycamore, cottonwood, silver maple, red maple, black willow and American elm. Trees more typical of mesic (mid-moisture) forests such as shagbark hickory and red oak may be found on floodplains, too. Ninebark, pussy willow and other willows, alders and swamp dogwood are typical floodplain shrubs. Floodwaters wash seeds and bulbs from upland forests down into the valleys, where they may establish themselves; thus many kinds of wildflowers, even those of the mountains which the streams drain, may be found in bloom in spring on floodplains soon after flood waters recede.

Dry Crests and Pine Barrens

Crest forests occur on the dry uplands of many river valleys, the dryness enhanced by the steep relief created by the rivers' history of erosion. This results in what might be paradoxically termed "low highlands" with quick

Red trillium (*Trillium erectum*)

28

drainage and high wind-stress. Typically, oaks reign in such contexts, most abundantly chestnut oak, with white oak, scarlet oak, black oak and post oak (in the southernmost parts of the Atlantic valleys) as associates. The driest of these ridge forests contain pine barrens elements such as the shrub-oaks (scrub oak and dwarf chestnut oak) and pitch pine. Indeed a few ridges, particularly in the Hudson Valley, are more pine barrens-like than oak ridge forest-like, being so dry that even the tree oaks find it hard to grow there. This trend reaches its extreme development in the dwarf pine barrens of the Shawangunk Mountains of southeastern New York State, one of only four dwarf pine forests in the entire Northeast. There are dwarf pine communities in New Jersey, on Long Island and in Rhode Island.

The pine barrens are the driest of the region's forests, some of them, as mentioned above, being dwarf forests of trees no more than head-high, often less. Nevertheless, they are forests, being dominated by a tree, pitch pine, although the co-dominant is a shrub (an oak, however) and even the pine trees are sometimes shrublike in size and form.

It seems evident that all the northeast's pine barrens are "offspring" of the New Jersey pine barrens, which remained free of ice during the entire Pleistocene (five glacial advances) and which are judged to be at least 20 million years old. After the ice left the land, seeds of pine barrens plants were carried (mostly by birds or on the wind) to places once occupied by ice. The ice had left many places favorable to dry-loving, sand-rooting plants, since the huge glacial lakes had all but disappeared, leaving the sands of their bottoms to drift dryly in the wind to form plains or dunes. The dry, glacially scoured ridges of the river valleys also played host to these hardy plants.

As soils developed and held more moisture, many of the post-glacial pine barrens gave way to mixed oak forests and then even to valley or northern hardwood forest. Those which remain have survived because the dry, nutrient-poor, high-acidity soils in which pine barrens plants thrive and avoid competition, have remained unchanged for thousands of years. This permanency has been maintained through the benefit of fires, which in dry habitats occur frequently and burn fast and shallowly,

Entoloma mushroom

29

Little bluestem grass (*Schizochireum scoparia*)

Jack-in-the-Pulpit (*Arisaema stewardsonii*)

leaving roots unscathed. Fire was a tool of the native peoples of the region, as mentioned before, and the region's pine barrens were certainly aided in their survival by the fires set by ancient peoples.

The modern policy of wildfire suppression has not been good for pine/oak barrens. Fire allows the pines, oaks and heath shrubs to survive, while killing invasive species such as poplars and black locust. Worse, the ease with which soil and vegetation can be removed has made pine barrens prime targets for development. This trend has been aggravated by the unfortunate location of most major pine barrens in places of dense human occupation, such as Long Island and Albany, New York. Strong efforts by conservationists have secured much of the remaining pine barrens acreage in the Northeast, but much of it was destroyed before anyone took an interest in it as an important natural resource. At the same time, field researchers keep finding "new" pine barrens, especially in recent years, in New England. They also report finding small remnants (a few pitch pines in a housing development, for example) of pine barrens now destroyed by residential or commercial development.

Swamp Forest

On the other end of the moisture scale are wet forests or swamps (technically, a swamp is a wooded wetland, as opposed to open wetlands such as bogs, marshes and fens). Most typical of the Northeast is the red maple swamp, a wetland dominated by one tree, the red maple. Tupelo and black ash may also be present, and especially in swamps which are part of river floodplain systems or near rivers, American elm, silver maple and sycamore.

An old red maple swamp is a lumpy place, the land occupied by the trees and by shrubs (most often highbush blueberry) raised a foot or more above the bottom of the swamp. This is most readily seen in late summer when the swamps often dry out completely. The trees and shrubs sit atop peaty hummocks formed around their roots, which can sometimes be seen where hollows have been eroded out. It looks as if the land has sunk over

Money plant (*Lunaria annua*)

the years, leaving the plants perched on their rootstocks, the roots having grown progressively lower to reach the sinking soil. What process of soil dynamics is at work in these swamps is an interesting question, but I have never read an account of such a process.

Forest Land Use

The forests of the Northeast have been greatly altered by logging and firewood harvesting, which cull particular species of trees from the forest. The original forests of the region were typically in a virgin state; few fires raged to wipe out huge tracts of woodlands except in pine barrens where fires are a natural part of the environmental regime, or in some of the larger river valleys where Indians burned off land to grow crops. Two of the first tree species to be harvested by Europeans were white pine for ships' masts and other building applications, and hemlock for the use of the bark in the tanning industry. In places where these two trees were abundant, such as the valleys and hollows of the Catskill Mountains, pine and hemlock were nearly wiped out, and today are still not nearly as abundant as they were.

Truly virgin forests exist today only in remote areas inaccessible to harvesting. More often than not natural stresses keep these undisturbed forests in a relatively poor condition, located as they often are, on high mountains exposed to wind, storm and cold. It takes a century or more for a forest to recover to a virgin appearance. Paradoxically, some of the

Collybia mushrooms

Calocera mushroom

Black swallow-wort (*Cynanchum nigrum*) on Yew (*Taxus*)

region's most long-protected forest tracts are located in or near urban areas, having been set aside by conservation-minded civic leaders in the early years of the nation's history. People in rural areas, being surrounded by trees, tended to think of them as resources or nuisances.

During this century, the devastation of forests has become a concern of environmentalists and state conservation agencies. Unfortunately, land use patterns and economic pressures often result in the devastation of a tract of pristine forest before it is acquired for preservation. Landowners typically have the tract logged and then sell it to the state, or timber companies donate land for preservation (a tax shelter) which has already been logged for profit. If these lands remain protected and if other threats (such as acid rain) don't damage them further, our descendants will inherit considerable acreage of old, healthy native forest.

NON-FOREST COMMUNITIES

Treeless environments are not typical of the Northeast. Most are artificial—cropland and pasture, lawn-like environments, formerly fire-maintained brushlands valued for their berry crops, roadsides, railways, power line cuts and other places where trees are periodically removed or vegetation chemically repressed. Oldfields, a very common habitat in the region, develop when agricultural habitat is no longer maintained. Once neglected, any artificial habitat soon becomes a richer place with new species invading year by year. Eventually, most such places revert to forest, but the process may take decades. The transition toward forest is called "succession" by "old-school" botanists, the term being applied to the stages of forest development from a young forest to a (presumably) stable old one, which is called a climax forest. Even lakes and ponds may eventually fill with sediments, becoming vegetated wetlands, then swamp forest and eventually a moderately moist mature forest.

Few natural open habitats occur in the region. The prairies of the midwest had a few small counterparts—the Hempstead plain on Long Island and a few similar grasslands in New England and on the Erie-

Ontario Lake Plain—but these have long been destroyed and developed. The remaining natural open lands are either wetlands or their opposite, habitats of open rock, very dry and nearly free of soil.

Wetlands

Open wetlands include marshes, bogs, fens and swales (wet grassy meadows). Marshes are characterized by open water and a muddy bottom, in which are rooted aquatic grasses and other plants which have a grass-like appearance. Such plants are called "emergents" because they stick up vertically from the water. Common aquatic grasses are cattails, giant reeds, reed canary grass, wild rice and rice cut-grass. Close relatives of grasses—rushes and sedges—are also abundant in marshes. Grass-like herbs include goldenclub, sweet flag and wild irises. Broad-leaved emergents include pickerelweeds and arrowheads. Floating-leaved plants such as water lilies and water-chestnut (a pest in the large rivers of the region) occur to a limited extent in marshes, but are more typical of ponds and lakes. Submerged plants include pondweeds, water-celery and water-milfoil.

Salt marshes are found in shallow bays and river deltas along the Atlantic Ocean. Many of these marshes are very disturbed or polluted, being located near large industrial complexes of the cities of the Atlantic coast. Salt marshes occur to a considerable distance up the Hudson River (to 60 miles north of New York City) and tidal marshes go up the river clear to the dam at Troy, 150 miles from New York City. The tidal oscillations greatly enhance the flow of nutrients in a marsh, so that tidal marshes are the most productive natural environments in terms of biomass output, the sheer amount of living matter created in the system. Fortunately, the Hudson River tidal marshes and other relatively undamaged coastal marshes are now under federal protection, although, being exposed to the open ocean and river waters, they are still subject to damage by pollution.

Inland fresh water marshes are uncommon. Since they are not subject to the tidal washes of coastal and estuarine marshes, inland marshes are

Pholiota mushrooms

Spider web in grasses

Fern "fiddleheads" (unrolling leaves)

often short-lived; soil accumulates, allowing shrubs and trees to move in. Fresh marshes may develop in abandoned loops of large streams or in glacially excavated hollows, such as the Great Vly on the border of Ulster and Greene counties in New York State. Still others are portions of wetland complexes which include other types of wetlands—bogs, swamps and swales. Examples include the great Cicero Swamp wetland complex and the offshore wetlands of the Ontario Lake Plain in New York State and southern Ontario.

The term "swale" typically refers to a moist grassy meadow without actual standing water. A fen is a limestone wetland characterized by low herbs (predominantly sedges and grasses) and shrubs, often cut through by small channels of cold, clear water from underground springs. A bog is an acidic wetland dominated by sphagnum moss, an almost aquatic moss with lush growth and very low nutrient requirements. These distinctions may not apply easily to large, complex wetlands where one type merges into another or where acidic and alkaline conditions are interspersed or layered one above the other.

Bogs

Bogs are wetlands of great antiquity, most having originated as standing waters in glacially-gouged potholes or kettle-shaped basins left when a large chunk of ice melted away. Over thousands of years, sphagnum moss has grown outward from the edge of the pond, leaving a legacy of peat.

Sphagnum mosses soak up many times their weight in moisture, can live without soil, and grow continually upon their own dead remains. The weight of this accumulation compacts the sphagnum into peat, forming a layer of this persistent, acidic material, often many meters in depth.

The moss also may grow outward toward the center of the pool to form a floating mat of sphagnum over the water.

In time, the bog mat may cover over the pond, so that it floats on the water invisible beneath it. A walker on such a bog will find the footing like a trampoline, as the mat undulates with each footstep. Eventually,

Mycena mushrooms

40

the peat builds up to fill the basin, so the bog at last becomes just a big soggy peat sponge. This may mark the beginning of the end, as by this stage, the bog's edges may have already begun to convert to shrubby wetland or swamp forest. But some bogs, in Maine especially, continue to mound up, remaining moist and free of tree intrusion for centuries. These raised bogs seem as stable as any mature forest.

In a bog, the rate of organic decay is so slowed by the high acidity that structures remain intact in the deep peat for hundreds—even thousands—of years. Some of these preserved objects make the news, such as the human corpses so well preserved in some European bogs. Also of scientific interest is plant pollen preserved in deep peat samples; since plant species can be identified by the shape of their pollen grains, ancient pollen from bogs gives a fairly accurate picture of past plant communities, soils and climates.

Besides sphagnum, bogs contain a wealth of other unusual plants, many found in no other kind of habitat. The sphagnum mat is typically so nutrient poor that only very specialized plants can survive in it. Bogs often have no source of water save natural precipitation, which unlike groundwater, bears little or no nutrient or mineral resources. Seacoast bogs receive some slight nutrient benefit from seaspray. Bog plants have evolved strategies for either conserving or doing without nutrients and minerals available in quantity to plants in richer habitats.

Carnivorous bog plants such as pitcher plants and sundews obtain minerals from the bodies of insects trapped by the plants' specialized leaves. Orchids are another group of plants whose members have evolved the ability to survive with little or no soil. Tropical orchids often grow on trees in rain forests where there is no problem getting daily moisture. In northern areas, orchids often live in bogs which provide similar conditions of low nutrients and high moisture.

The high acidity of some bogs is ameliorated by their being perched atop limestone bedrock. Limestone imparts an alkaline condition to the soils as calcium carbonate is dissolved out of the bedrock. Deeply rooted plants of alkaline affinity may grow along with the usual acid-loving bog plants. If you find both white cedar and tamarack, or both sundews and

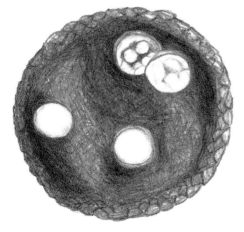

Bird's nest fungus (*Crucibulum*) in acorn cap.

Phaeocollybia mushroom

Williams Lake, Rosendale, New York

grass-of-parnassus, in a wetland, you know it has both alkaline and acid soil horizons. A high complement of lime-loving plants makes a wetland a fen rather than a bog, but the distinction is often blurred in reality.

Bogs are fairly long-lived phenomena, but they are fragile and can't take a lot of trampling. Fortunately (in this regard at least) they are not especially popular places. Bogs are rare and usually located in areas far from dense human populations.

Some bogs in the Northeast have been acquired by conservation groups or state agencies, and these are sometimes open to the public. In such soggy places, to facilitate visitors and to protect fragile plants, trails or boardwalks are often constructed, making access easier and protecting the bog from trampling, but compromising the sense of wildness. Nevertheless, these public bogs are of tremendous interest to beginning botanists, providing a good introduction to some of the region's most fascinating plant communities.

Lakes and streams are often too deep or too fast-moving to support much plantlife. The best places to find aquatic plants are ponds, quiet shallow lakes, wetlands with open water and sluggish streams. Water lilies may cover the surface of a pond, or the waters may erupt in a bright display of yellow or white bladderwort blossoms in June. Most other aquatic plants remain hidden beneath the water, and are best examined in a well-lit aquarium, since when taken out of water they typically fall limp and formless.

Slabrock Communities

Bedrock in the Northeast usually lies below several inches to several or many feet of soil, but there are places where soil failed to build up after the glaciers scoured the rocks of the region thousands of years ago. Such bare rock habitats are kept from gathering a blanket of soil by one or more unusual conditions. Incessant winds on high crests may dry out and blow away most of the small organic fragments that would eventually become soil. A very large bedrock plateau may only slowly develop soil along its fringes. A pitched flatrock exposure may continually lose debris with soil potential to the washing action of rains.

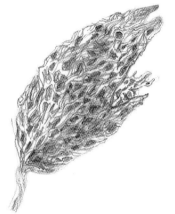

Wild cucumber (*Echinocystis lobata*) seedpod husk.

Most of the bedrock exposures in the area are the elevated type, and not especially large. These ledge or ridge habitats can be found in nearly all mountainous parts of the region, or in districts with low, rocky hills. Often the passage of the glaciers has enhanced the ruggedness of such areas, maximizing the acreage of such habitat. Bedrock environments of many angles and aspects occur, from level ledges to steeply angled exposures of geologic synclines and anticlines, to vertical cliff faces. This variety of landforms fosters a corresponding diversity of plant communities, which include among their member species many rare and beautiful flowering plants and a number of rare plants dull and plain to the uninitiated, but of great interest and concern to botanists and professional conservationists.

It is in these places that the influence of geology on plants is most tangible. Lichens are usually the first plants to establish themselves on bare rock. These tiny plants appear as flakes, chips or antler-like structures, are very brittle in dry weather and crumble under the feet of animals or people. These loose fragments can blow off and reattach themselves to rocks some distance away. In addition, the lichens produce spores which blow even further on the wind. Lichens are dual organisms, a partnership of an alga and a fungus. This symbiosis has been touted by some writers as unique among plants, but in fact, such partnerships are the rule among green plants and fungi, not the exception, as we will see when we examine the native mushrooms in the later summer section of this book.

Mosses are the next plants to move in where lichens have softened the rock with their acid secretions and have built pockets of wetter crude soil (lichen powder and rock particles). Later still, herbs and grasses adapted to dry, shallow soils will enter the most developed pockets or root into cracks in the rock where soil has accumulated. In large fissures of flat rock plains, even trees and shrubs will grow, but they will be sparsely distributed and often stunted by the lack of nutrients and the restricted root space of the rock crevices.

Large rock plains are known as pavement barrens, and such habitats are rare throughout the world. There are several in the Northeast. These include the serpentine barrens of Pennsylvania and the Pocono pine

Insect gall on grapevine.

45

Tuliptree (*Liriodendron tulipifera*) leaves

Honeysuckle (*Lonicera*) berry

barrens which lie just south of the glacial terminus, and in the glaciated Northeast, the grand Limerick Cedars and Lyme Prairie limestone barrens in New York's Jefferson County, the greatest pavement barrens acreage in the country and host to seven rare plant species. Other pavement barrens occur in the Maritime provinces and in southern Ontario.

Mountain balds and summits are similar to pavement barrens, but are even more highly specialized, due to the extreme stresses of wind and cold that prevail at high elevations. Mountain plant communities experience a truncated growing season compared with that of lowland communities. Growth and reproduction is restricted to the summer months, so mountaintop plants are discussed in more detail in Chapter Three.

Disturbed Communities

More commonly, the places we go for natural solace or adventure are those bearing the marks of our own current or past use—the neglected weedy corners of towns and cities or the back acres of farms or our own back yards. Such habitats provide a mix of native and foreign plants, the immigrant species usually far outnumbering the natives. In the most disturbed places, such as road edges, there are often no native plants in the flora. One native plant which competes well in disturbed places is common milkweed, which mingles happily with wild parsnip, wild carrot, bouncing bet, bladder campion, rough-fruited cinquefoil, viper's bugloss and the rest of the "wretched refuse" of Eurasian weeds.

Between the shrubs grow grasses, perennial and annual forbs, and in some dry upland oldfields, bracken and boulder ferns. Moisture gradients are reflected in plant species composition. In dry soils grow gray dogwood, choke cherry, sweet-fern, bluestem and hair-grasses, and flowering herbs such as pussytoes, everlastings, hawkweeds and knapweeds. Shrubs of moist oldfields include silky dogwood, smooth and speckled alders, meadowsweet and blackberry. The herb flora is incredibly diverse and is discussed in Parts Three and Four.

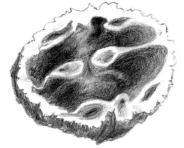

Black walnut (*Juglans nigra*) half, opened by squirrel.

Some disturbed habitats are chronically redisturbed, and thus kept from developing along their natural courses. Roadsides and hayfields are periodically mowed, so they remain what they are botanically until the mowing stops. When the mowing (or plowing or grazing) does stop, interesting things happen. Plants which couldn't survive the chronic disturbance begin to enter the habitat, diversity increases, and usually the vegetation becomes taller season after season. Shrubs and young trees sprout up here and there, and the former hayfield or cow pasture becomes that most familiar of rural wild habitats, the oldfield.

Some oldfields remain as they are for many decades, while others quickly revert to young forest. I believe the speed of succession reflects land use history and soil quality; for example: trees grow poorly in dense clay soils, the dense grasses of old pastures discourage seeds from sprouting, and the forest fungi on which trees depend are usually absent from soils in which trees have not grown for many years (the dependence is mutual).

Oldfields, though free of trees, are often dotted with shrubs. Common oldfield shrubs are red cedar, several small dogwoods and viburnums, sweet-fern and choke cherry. Black cherry occurs in two forms, as a large forest tree or a small oldfield treelet. The oldfield form grows hardly at all beyond a height of a few meters. The eastern tent caterpillar relentlessly prunes oldfield cherries, and there may be other environmental influences that keep these trees small. Probably the two forms are also genetically distinct.

Lichen (*Cetraria*) on twig.

49

SPRING

FOR many reasons spring is the favorite season of many people. The sudden relief from the cold of winter and its attendant rigors and labors, the spectacle of new green buds and colorful blossoms, the arrival of migrant birds from the south—all these and other aspects of nature's warm awakening combine to make spring an especially seductive season. Only autumn rivals spring in terms of grand visual changes. Spring has the added attraction of a long summer ahead of it.

In considering the seasons biologically, calendar dates at best approximate the loose timing of natural processes. Even the most well-known events of spring—the robins' arrival, the blooming of crocuses, the perambulation of amphibian multitudes on a rainy night—take place on different dates in different places, and on different dates from year to year. Every spring is different: some are late, some early; some wet, some dry; some smooth and even, others marked by violent shifts of weather swinging from summery spells to wintry freezes. The most extreme sort of spring can be dangerous.

I recall one spring that came dangerously early with three weeks of very warm weather beginning in late March. Tender new leaves and fragile flowers dressed the landscape in Easter magnificence. Then frost struck hard in the third week of April; temperatures dove into the teens one night. Next morning the tender green leaves had been freezer-burned like those of garden peppers and tomatoes after a late fall frost; magnolia flowers looked scorched. In a few days these sorry leaves and flowers fell away, and it was not until late May when the late-leafing trees began to awaken that the landscape began to regreen itself. The plants that were frosted survived, but did not refoliate until mid-June.

Even in the best of springs, some species of plants leaf or bloom later than others, so that the entire sequence of greening spans a period five to seven weeks in any particular location. Within the Northeast as a whole, spring comes as early as March in the warmest parts of the region, and may not give way to summer until late June in the coldest parts. In areas with both low valleys and high mountains, spring may extend over this entire time span.

Though the time spring begins may vary, there is very little variation in

Skunk cabbage (*Symplocarpus foetidus*)

Previous pages: Spring trees

the sequence of blooming and leafing of the plant species in a particular environment or geographic area. Having kept lists of blooming wildflowers for fifteen years, I can attest to this rigidity of sequence. Skunk cabbage is always first; hepatica and coltsfoot vie for second; trailing arbutus is almost always the third flower to bloom unless it's beaten out by lyre-leaved rock cress. After that, quite a few plants set blossoms, and it becomes a matter of which ones you find first. The same holds true for leaves: bush honeysuckle and barberry are first, followed by maples, cherries, poplars, birches and willows; elms follow and then oaks and finally locusts.

Another pattern is to be found in plants of different sizes; in general, smaller plants become active in spring before larger ones do. The ground thaws from the top down, so moisture and dissolved nutrients first become available in the upper layers of the soil. Shallow-rooted plants are the first to tap into these newly-freed resources. Watch the grass in April; it's the fastest growing vegetation in early spring.

Trees are a special case. Being so large and deeply rooted, they can tap into resources below the frostline. There are few nutrients in these deep parts of soil, but there is plenty of water, and the trees have stored sugar in abundance from the growing season before. As soon as the sun warms dark tree trunks well above freezing, the sap starts to flow. Maple syrup makers know this; that's why in rural parts of the Northeast tap buckets can be seen on sugar maples well before the snow has completely melted away, in March or even in February.

Even though trees begin activity very early in spring, they do not produce leaves for a month or more after the sap begins to flow. Trees, being relatively huge plants, require more time than small plants to get their life processes operating to the point of building leaves; most trees also flower and even set seed before their leaves are fully expanded. This sluggishness of trees allows the smaller plants time to bloom in the sun before the leaves of trees shade the ground.

The lack of leaves on the larger trees of the forest is one of the most important ecological considerations of spring. Sun is available everywhere except in dense evergreens. In early spring the forest is warmer than the

Pussy willow (*Salix discolor*)

53

Rose twisted-stalk (*Streptopus roseus*)

Bloodroot (*Sanguinea canadensis*)

open field; trees absorb heat with their dark trunks and slowly radiate this heat to the air at night when frost is still a threat to small plants. Trees also act as windbreaks to reduce "wind chill." For the most part, more flowering plants bloom earlier in woodlands than in open places. An exception is coltsfoot, one of the earliest bloomers of spring, a plant which prefers roadsides and open banks of slumping soil.

The warmth of spring is not spread around evenly. Heat tends to collect in little pockets warmed by the sun and protected from the wind. Sunless or windswept locations are cold, and there spring will be delayed. South-facing slopes are warm because they face the low-angled spring sun most directly. The difference this makes can be seen during a drive in hilly country on a sunny day in late winter before the snow has melted. South slopes will stand out because of their lack of snow; the stronger sun there will have melted it away while it remains in other places. North slopes are cold and snow melts late there. The climate may be so much colder than that of south slopes that entirely different plant species grow there.

Climatic conditions differ also along the same slope, especially if it's a long one such as the shank of a mountain. At the bottom, conditions are more extreme than at midslope; cold air sinks into the valley at night while warm air from the valley rises upslope in the evening keeping frost at bay in the midslope region. High places—ridges and peaks—are simply colder, being exposed to high winds and the cooler air of higher layers of the atmosphere. This cooling with higher elevation continues without limit to the point where in high mountains, spring may be delayed by a month or more.

Other nuances of small scale biogeography affect the progress of spring from one place to another. One is the presence of ice in such habitats as wooded swamps and ponds and marshes. Ice reflects sunlight, absorbs little heat,and so is a persistent cooling agent. Dark objects embedded in ice speed its melting, as does any flow of water beneath it and around it (or over it, as happens at times of flooding). Large trees with dark trunks are quite effective at melting ice. Even a leaf on the ice will heat up and sink through, eventually making a hole to water. One common swamp

Round-lobed hepatica
(*Hepatica americana*)

tree of the northeast, pin oak, fails to drop its leaves in autumn. They are wrenched off by winter winds and fall upon the snow and ice of the frozen swamp. It's interesting to speculate that pin oak strains which delayed leaf-drop gained an advantage over "quick-droppers" by getting a head start in spring by melting swamp ice with leaves.

Available moisture is an important influence on the growth of plants in spring. Plants in dry habitats are slow to grow since their moisture (and thus their nutrients, which are water-borne) is in short supply. A very dry plant community such as a pine/oak barren may be as warm or warmer in spring than other habitats, but still be slower to go green because of the very dry conditions there.

Habits of long-standing die as hard in plants as they do in people. Many of the plants we see outdoors regularly are not native species and they have become adapted to conditions unlike the ones prevailing in northeastern North America. The weeping willow and Norway maple are good examples. The first is Chinese and its habit of leafing out early and staying green later than any other common tree (except perhaps the European white birch) reflects its native home with a similarly cold winter but a longer growing season. Norway maple leafs with its near-relatives among the native trees, but stays green much longer in the fall, reflecting an adaptation to a northern coastal climate where the sea's influence delays spring warming and fall cooling. Remember too that foreign trees are adapted to a different photoperiod regime, and this may override responses to weather.

More often than not the smell of spring is the first thing that announces its arrival. That smell is the mix of gases exuded by billions of microorganisms newly active in the soil, yet we can't help interpreting it as the freshest smell in the world. The soil has come to life, and so can the flowers and leaves be far behind?

Flowers reign in spring as in no other season and there's a good reason. Flowers, once pollinated, lead to seeds, and seeds need time to develop. Furthermore, there is considerable competition among plants to populate the world with their offspring. The first ones to enter the seed race are often the winners, though there are other ways of winning.

Bloodroot (*Sanguinea canadensis*)

Spring brings a rush of forest flowers rather than those of the open fields, the wetlands, brushlands, sand barrens and shores. Here, too, we find good reason. Recalling the size factor, it's easy to see that small plants can beat the trees in the race to be green or to bloom. Not only can they, but they must. Once the trees leaf out the forest floor becomes a darker place, the warm, bright sun largely shut out by the lush canopy of leaves. Nearly all the herbs of the forest floor bloom in the warm period just before the leaves of trees expand.

One plant beats all the rest to blooming. The skunk cabbage has a singularly unflowerlike blossom, a thick, tough, fibrous sheath shaped like a fat flame sheltering an unassuming cluster of small yellowish blossoms, the true flowers. The flame-like form is appropriate to the plant's strange power, unique among our flora, to generate so much heat that it literally melts its way up through frozen ground and snow to bloom in February or March. Skunk cabbage prefers non-acid soils of swampy lowlands, especially black muck, truck-farming soil. In such habitats the maroon or yellow-green speckled flames can be found at the end of winter, each in its little cup of bare ground ringed by the snow which its heat has driven back.

The skunk cabbage is a blessing to those cabin-feverish nature lovers weary of winter, a loved object even with its foetid odor and contingent of buzzing flies. These overwintering flies are the only pollinators available at this early season, and since they are not nectar-feeders but rely on the newly thawed carcasses of dead animals, the flies would not be attracted to a sweet smell. Sweet-smelling flowers that draw bees and butterflies are still a month away.

When at last the snow melts to a vanishing patchwork, the upper soil layers become free of ice, soil microorganisms begin to release nutrients and fungal hyphae resume the function of gathering distant mineral resources for their green plant symbiotes, and in the few inches above last fall's old leaves the air lies warm and thick upon the ground—only then do the herbs of the woods spring to life after the long winter sleep. After a week or so of balmy weather, the first spring flowers appear.

The forest wildflower community presents one of the most beautiful

Marsh marigold (*Calthra palustris*)

Early saxifrage (*Saxifraga virginiensis*)   Squirrel corn (*Dicentra canadensis*)

flower shows to be seen anywhere. There are hundreds of species of flowers in the various forest communities of the Northeast, and probably close to 90% of these bloom in the spring. Each type of forest contains a different array of flowers, and within each forest system, wildflower assemblages vary with environmental conditions. Some forests are far richer in spring wildflowers than others because of especially favorable conditions there. Adequate moisture, rich soil, sunny exposure and protection from grazers (especially deer) usually guarantee good flower hunting. The bases of cliffs, stream banks, outwash plains (places where water spreads out in a fan shape, slows down and drops lightweight debris), and talus slopes (slowly moving piles of rock and soil at the bases of cliffs) in mountainous country are especially rich in wildflowers. Some stream floodplains are productive as well. Limestone imparts an alkalinity to soils when the limestone is dissolved or when fragments of the stone make up a portion of the soil itself. Such "sweet soils" favor calcicoles, lime-loving plants, many of which flower in spring.

There is a rough order to the appearance of various species of wildflowers. The first wave of bloom includes but a few species. Hepatica is usually the first woodland herb to bloom, while at the same time in disturbed soils such as mudslides, gravel banks and shale piles the dandelion-like flowers of coltsfoot, an alien plant, appear. Examination reveals the stalks of both plants to be covered with tiny hairs, making them appear furry. Like the fur of animals, this downiness protects the plants from frost. But where with animals the coat holds in body heat, with these plants, the hairs make ice condensation practically impossible.

A third early bloomer, trailing arbutus, boasts pink or white bell-like blossoms at the ends of trailing stems which hug the ground and often lie beneath last year's leaves. Arbutus is right on the heels of hepatica, which may bloom nearby, but arbutus is slower to open its buds and usually blooms a few days after hepatica's first opening. This plant is highly opportunistic, seeding into slight disturbances in its native dry oak woods, old logging roads, places where firewood has been harvested, or recovering edges of more intense disturbances such as shale mines or stone quarries. Behind our house there is a quarry road part of which is cut more deeply

Early saxifrage (*Saxifraga virginiensis*)

60

into the land to leave slowly eroding banks on either side. Over the last six years, trailing arbutus has increased dramatically along this path, both in number and size of the plants. Since it is a plant of dry, thinly treed forests, probably fire has aided its proliferation in the past. Its fondness for woodland paths is a boon to the plant-hunter, making it among the easiest of spring flowers to locate, once you learn to recognize its ground-hugging, leathery leaves and pink or white blossoming bells.

Recognizing plants before they bloom is a valuable skill, since then a person can explore the woods in the weeks before the spring flower explosion begins, and locate rich gardens before the show begins. In the midst of mid-spring it is inevitable to come across flowers already wilted and going to seed, but such disappointments can be minimized by some advance scouting.

Even though various spring blossoms first open at progressive stages of the season, most remain in bloom long enough that many kinds of flowers can be seen at once. Thus, hepatica, alone in the woods for a few days, is joined as it reaches its stage of richest flower, by other neighbors—rue anemone, early saxifrage, bloodroot, trout lily, dutchman's breeches, miterwort, smooth rock cress, early buttercup and several kinds of violet.

This list is just one possible array. Each plant has a range of conditions in which it will live, but these conditions may overlap or occur in very close proximity to the conditions favored by other plants. A varied terrain presents the best chance of finding a variety of floral arrays. Pick an area with rock exposures, low moist areas, higher plateaus, slopes facing different directions, and waters of several kinds—a stream, a swamp, a vernal pool (one which is filled with water only in spring), a permanent pond or lake. Because of its often rugged but not too extreme geology and topographic relief, the Northeast abounds in good wildflower country.

An early walk in low country is a good plan. Spring comes late to the highlands, but in the river valleys or the lowlands in the vicinity of large lakes or the ocean, spring gets a head start. These are the areas of long growing seasons. The major ones include coastal New England, the Erie-Ontario Lake Plain, the Finger Lakes region, and the larger river

Rue anemone (*Anemonella thalictroides*)

Hair-cap moss (*Polytrichum juniperinum*)

Moss (*Bryum caespiticium*)

valleys—the Hudson, Connecticut, Delaware/Susquehanna, Housatonic and Penobscot. The St. Lawrence/Lake Champlain lowlands, though located in the northern part of the region, are for that part of the Northeast relatively warm.

In the warmer parts of the region, late April or early May is usually prime time for woodland wildflowers. The earliest ones can still be found in bloom and by that time many other plants are in prime bloom or beginning to open blossoms. The vicinity of a stream through rocky terrain is an excellent place to look for wildflowers. At the edge of a country road, an old logging road heads into the woods. The buds of shrubs such as bush honeysuckle and barberry are already opening to add green baby leaves to the red of last fall's berries still clinging to their twigs. In the swampy floodplain of the stream the spicebush is in full bloom, its every branch laced with tiny yellow-green flowers that fill the air with a subtle perfume. In this sluggish part of the stream, big dots of yellow catch the walker's eye. These are the blooms of marsh marigold, a woodland emergent aquatic which roots along the banks of slow streams and their backwater pools. On the flat, silty sediments of the stream banks grow trout lilies, not as obvious as the big golden marsh marigolds, but fully as attractive in a more subdued way.

The outwash plain bears further investigation. There, thrusting through the new silt of a March flood is a troupe of bloodroot, just a day or two out as shown by the single deeply-lobed, coarse-veined leaf still embracing the stem of the flower, now advanced above this protective sheath of a leaf and open starlike to the warm spring sun. These first bloodroots will be joined in the following days by others still beneath the sediments. Their flowers last only a few days, and each plant bears only one.

The bark of a big tree attracts the eye, strangely mottled in pastels of beige and olive, in places flaking off in great curled chips. It is a great sycamore, a tree of stream floodplains that likes its roots soaking wet most of the time. And in the lee of the sycamore's trunk, shielded from racing floodwaters, grows a spectacular flower. With its huge three-lobed leaves and luxuriant three-sepaled maroon flowers, it looks more like something from a flower shop than a wild thing. It's a red trillium, and a very old

Shadbush (*Amelanchier arborea*)

64

specimen, protected by the big tree for perhaps thirty years or more. Whereas most trilliums are one-leaved, one-flowered affairs, this one is like a bounteous bouquet of such lesser examples. Count the stalks and blossoms. There are sixteen flowers open and seven more buds about to break—twenty-three separate flowering stalks from one base! A super-trillium indeed.

A yard from the trillium there's a large cluster of similarly three-lobed leaves, dark maroonish green. This is a different plant surely, with its scalloped leaflets and on just a few specimens clusters of flower buds. Further along there's one just in bloom showing white, four-petaled flowers, the mark of the mustard family. This is toothwort, and its mustardness is revealed also in its taste. Pick a leaf and chew it, and you'll be treated to a taste quite like its more familiar relative, horseradish. The young leaves, gathered sparingly so as not to weaken the plants, make a spicy addition to a salad.

Another white flower strikes the wanderer's eye, and closely examined proves to have a most whimsical shape, that of a pair of white, baggy sailor's pants hung upside-down to dry on a line. From this appearance comes its name, dutchman's breeches. Its leaves are lovely, too—pale blue-green, fragile and lacy like those of maidenhair fern.

On the other side of the path, the land rises to the bottom of a ledge of gray, weathered rock, a limestone exposure, part of a long accumulation of mineral and organic sediments laid down 330 million years earlier in a shallow sea. In the talus (rock debris) at the base of the cliff grow more bloodroot plants, and with them a slender, downy plant with two maple-like leaves joining the stalk at its middle, and rising above these paired leaves, an uncurling stalk of delicate floral snowflakes. This plant is miterwort, a lover of rich, neutral soils.

On the rock face flowers grow from cracks and hollows where soil has accumulated. One such plant bears four-petalled white flowers like those of the toothwort of the floodplain, but this is a long, lean plant with thin leaves, the lyre-leaved rock cress. In talus where the limestone has crumbled off we find its relative, the smooth rock cress with its bell-like yellow-green flowers. The petals are partly fused and so are not readily

Wild ginger (*Asarum canadense*)

65

Trailing arbutus (*Epigaea repens*)   Miterwort (*Mitella diphylla*)

Long-spurred violet (*Viola rostrata*)

recognized as mustard flowers. Also in this talus are wild columbines with red and yellow chandelier-like flowers.

Along the crest of the ledge the long rays of the afternoon sun cast long shadows. One shadow is a thin, straight line. The thing casting this shadow is a cable bolted to a hornbeam tree. Growing along the cable is a slender vine with pale yellow-green leaves and big lavender flowers that look as if they're made of crepe paper or some sort of glittery fabric. They sparkle back-lit by the sinking sun, by far the most spectacular flowers on the limestone ledge. This plant is the wild purple clematis, a rare relative of garden clematises.

A large crack in the rock has filled with soil to form a sloping passage to the plateau atop the limestone slab. At the edge of the small cliff grow early saxifrage plants, the leaves at their bases like succulent hearts and their flowers like tiny cauliflower heads. In a crack of this rocky ledge we find a wild violet of pale lavender with a deep blue-violet center. A close look reveals the long spur extending behind the open blossom. This is the long-spurred violet, one of the few violets which branches in its growth (most have leaves and flowers emanating from a central stock).

Behind the cliff edge the land is still rocky, but here trees and shrubs have taken root in rock crevices to form a sparsely wooded plain. The dominant trees are chinkapin oak and hop-hornbeam with large sugar maples at intervals where some large fissure affords ample root room. From shrubs beneath this thin canopy dangle a few curious papery pods which rattle in the breeze. These big brown seed pouches give this lime-loving bush its name, bladdernut. The bladdernut bushes have just begun to open pale green buds, which in a week or two will trail off in dangling bell-like blossoms buzzing with bees. On the forest floor we find hepatica in abundance, and in all its color forms—white, pink, blue and violet. The fragile rue anemones shiver in the slightest breeze, their pink-fringed white blossoms nodding to and fro. A darker violet stands out against the brown leaves of last autumn. Its leaves are shaped like hands. This is the lime-loving early blue violet. A few yards away we notice another early blue with a yellow companion. Its shape indicates that it too is a violet, and its hairiness proves it to be the downy yellow violet. There are also white violets but we shall meet them in other places.

Canada violet (*Viola canadensis*)

One is not far off as it turns out. East of the rock plain, the land drops gently down through deeper woods. Here there are almost no flowers; the leaves lie dense upon the level ground undisturbed by the winds that buffet the plateau above. But a few hundred paces northeast we come to a small opening in the forest, a tiny patch of limestone wetland, a mini-fen. The cold water of this little boggy spot slows down growth, but one flower is just opening its tiny maroon-centered white blossoms—a small colony of the rare lance-leaved white violet grows in the sphagnum moss at the edge of the fen, down among sedges where the blossoms are almost invisible.

Past the fen the original path curves around to the north and then climbs westward, leaving the limestone strata to cross over soils underlain by sandstones and shales. The difference is apparent to the botanist, even though the geologist (because the rocks that form the basis of that study are buried beneath the earth) might not tell the change had taken place. The chinkapin oak has been replaced here by chestnut oak and scarlet oak, with an occasional white oak. One of these white oaks is a giant, four feet in diameter with a wide, spreading crown. The other oaks here are narrow in their branching and dwarfs by comparison. This land was once a pasture, with the single large oak left to provide shelter for the grazing sheep or cattle.

Flowers are absent in the vicinity of the big oak, the ground plants there being grasses and sedges and among them the early leaves of fall-blooming asters. Just beyond what was once a pasture is another old trail, probably an old farm road, and here there are flowers, little four-petalled blue blossoms on short stalks with small leaves. These are bluets, often mistaken for forget-me-nots. As the path moves downslope through denser woods of young oaks, hemlocks and mountain laurel (in early bud), another spring flower makes its appearance. This is a ground creeper with evergreen foliage, a heath that likes acid soils, the trailing arbutus. Its tight packet of pink blossoms pokes out from under a big red oak leaf. Lifting the leaf we find the tough blunt-oblong leaves of the plant, shining with minute, stiff hairs. Along the path we find half a dozen arbutus plants, one directly in the center of the trail, a sprawling giant a meter in diameter.

Squirrel corn (*Dicentra canadensis*)

Showy orchis (*Orchis spectabilis*)

Wood anemone (*Anemone quinquefolia*)

A very different kind of spring hike awaits the explorer of mountainous country. Because spring is delayed with increasing elevation, climbing a mountain becomes a journey backward in time, the season becoming earlier as one ascends the mountain. A mountain hike should be undertaken after spring has developed for several weeks down in the valleys; only then will there be enough of the mountain in active spring blooming and growth to make the climb worthwhile.

At the base of the mountain, dutchman's breeches, bloodroot, red trillium and other early-blooming flowers have passed the blooming stage and show the beginnings of seed pod development. Later flowers such as Virginia waterleaf and tall meadow rue are coming into bloom. Trees are half leafed out and in a matter of days the forest floor will be mostly shaded over. But higher up the mountain slope, conditions are increasingly "earlier" in terms of vegetative development.

Only 500 feet higher than the starting point, the dutchman's breeches are just in very early leaf. Under them grow Canada violets in profusion, big plants half a foot tall with multiple blooms of purple and white. A bit beyond the beech grove where sugar maples take over, smooth yellow violets form a bed that blends with the Canada violet in rich mountain woods. Of all the violets of the Northeast, these two are the biggest plants and have the longest blooming season, from mid-spring into mid-summer.

At 1200 feet from our point of origin (an elevation of 2300 feet, since we began at a valley level of 1100) beech reappears along with hemlock and yellow birch. Here the soil is rich, but fairly acidic and somewhat peaty. Spring beauties are still in bloom here, while their counterparts on the valley stream floodplain have already set seed. The wild lily of the valley and the starflower are blooming here, and on stonier ground upslope, the wood anemone in the talus and old leaves. Where the path becomes clay we find a new violet between the exposed roots of a big sugar maple. It's a yellow one with dark green downy leaves with a glossy sheen like those of an African violet. This is the round-leaved violet, a denizen of cool mountain slopes forested with northern hardwoods, white pine and hemlock. In summer its leaves grow huge and round to catch whatever spattering of sun breaks through the high canopy.

Blue cohosh (*Caulophyllum thalictroides*)

At the end of a steep climb there is a gently sloping terrace cut by numerous small streams emanating from springs breaking out of the mountain bedrock behind the slope. Boulders of all sizes are strewn about the woods here, an old woodland of tall sugar maples, basswoods, white ash, white pine and butternut, indicators of deep, rich soil. In front of a big boulder is a natural flower bed, a wild garden of waving white. These flowers are very like the dutchman's breeches encountered on the floodplain a few weeks before, but not so creamy, a purer white, and are of a rounder shape. This plant is a close relative of dutchman's breeches, squirrel corn, a plant of cooler climes, but not so biased in its habitat selection that the two are always found apart. Not fifty yards away along a little freshet the two grow together.

A closer look reveals that these flowers are each nipped at one lobe of the white heart, and there is not a perfect blossom in the hundreds here. A droning bumblebee alights in the center of the patch and commences chewing on a blossom with only one lobe disfigured, completing the damage begun by an earlier bee visitor. Only small bees can get at the nectar through the flower's opening; the big ones can't fit and so they just break in, wrecking the flowers. This can be very frustrating for flower photographers.

In a flat, soggy place along the path of the freshet stream grows a plant akin to the miterwort of the limestone talus of the lowlands. Its leaves are hairier and it bears a cluster of greenish, starlike flowers on a downy stalk. Foamflower, like miterwort, is a member of the saxifrage family. In this spring seep is found another member of this family, a plant resembling the early saxifrage of limestone cliffs, but much larger, Pennsylvania saxifrage.

Across the freshet the land climbs gently and hemlock increases, shading the ground even at this early season. In the dappled shade grows a tiny white violet, one of two very similar species, both lovers of cool, moist acid woodlands. Though hard to distinguish in flower, they can be identified when the seed capsules form later in the summer; northern white violet has a green seed case while that of sweet white violet is purplish.

Painted trillium (*Trillium undulatum*)

73

Red trillium (*Trillium erectum*)

Yellow lady-slipper (*Cypripedium calceolus*)

The land levels out for a time, leading past a small wooded swamp. At the edge of the water are trilliums, but not the red species. These are painted trilliums with olive to maroonish leaves and maroon-centered white blooms, flowers of cooler, damper woods than those preferred by red trillium. Red trillium is in this neighborhood, too, on slightly drier ground up the path, and both trilliums will be encountered all the way up the mountain.

On a drier terrace, beech trees outnumber all other species (wild black cherry, yellow birch, sugar maple, hop-hornbeam) combined. The ground in front of a big glacially deposited boulder is covered with five-petalled candy-striped flowers, spring beauties. There are two kinds. This is Carolina spring beauty, as told by its wider leaves and fondness for drier habitats than the thin-leaved Virginia spring beauty. Hepatica pops up here, too, but these hepatica plants have pointed leaves, whereas the hepaticas of the limestone ledges had blunt leaves and a more compact form. Botanists disagree as to whether these two forms are separate species or varieties of one species.

At higher elevations, the plants are in earlier and earlier stages of development. There is a point where the squirrel corn plants are just in early bud, their lacy leaves still timidly folded against the cooler conditions and delayed spring of the higher elevation. Still higher, just above a steep 50-foot cliff the land is cold and windswept, with no sign of greening and with lingering snow in the shade of boulders. Spring will not arrive here for another two weeks.

A mountain hike will reveal how spring moves slowly uphill as the weather grows warmer and warmer. Should you have a view of a mountain from your home or along an oft-traveled road, keep an eye on the mountain from the time buds begin to open in the valley. You'll see a green wave move up the mountain slope over the next few weeks. When it nears the top, return to the mountain and hike to the summit where spring will be fresh, though it may have passed already at valley level.

On the mountaintops where spring comes last of all, there may be completely different flowers from those found on the lower slopes. The trees, shrubs and ferns will also be different. On the very highest

Jack-in-the-Pulpit (*Arisaema stewardsonii*)

mountains of the region, there are no trees, and even the shrubs are stunted on the cold, windswept peaks. The flora here is of an arctic-alpine type which may include elements found hundreds of miles to the north in the Canadian tundra, as well as plants adapted only to high mountain summits and ridges above treeline (true alpines). Here, spring may not come until summer comes to the valley.

Most mountains of the Northeast are forested on their upper reaches by some variant of Canadian conifer forest or, if conditions are dry, a "Canadian" forest without the conifers, consisting of deciduous species often found in association with spruce and fir. High elevation forests are usually weather stressed and often sparsely wooded, leaving openings for ferns and flowering plants. In such a place in late spring the plant hunter would likely encounter corn lily (Clinton's lily), twisted-stalk or rose twisted-stalk, goldthread, mountain wood sorrel (in shady glades) and bunchberry, a dwarfed dogwood that looks like a plucked single flower of flowering dogwood.

Herbaceous wildflowers tend to overshadow another group of spring blossoms—those of the forest trees. The catkins of the pussy willow are the tree flowers most familiar to people, but many other trees have flowers sufficiently attractive to be worth examining. Blooming with the willows very early in the season are "soft" maples (red and silver maples) and poplars. The latter have catkins similar to willows. Maple flowers are red to yellow in color and, though small, add up to the magnificent display in a swamp forest where maples are the dominant trees. In March or April (May in the north) maple flowers turn the woods a misty red against blue-gray trunks. Mingled with the yellows of maturing willow flowers, the landscape assumes a wash of gentle but vivid new color.

It is worthwhile to visit the same site at intervals of a week to ten days to keep an eye on the progress of spring. Plants which were not yet in bloom on the previous visit will be attractively blossoming on the next excursion. Returning to the limestone ledge area a week or so later when the leaves of the trees are open just enough to give the landscape a pointillistic look, we will find another set of plants to enjoy.

Two weeks later many of the plants that had been in bloom then have

Perfoliate bellwort (*Uvularia perfoliata*)

77

gone to seed: the marsh marigolds in the stream have nearly all shed their yellow petals and the green fruits are beginning to swell; bloodroot leaves are now nearly saucer-sized, paired with swelling seed capsules on long stalks like a butterfly's antennae; the saxifrages on the ledges have grown long, droopy and ragged. Other plants such as rock cresses and columbine are more florific than before, the older flowers having begun to produce fruit, but new flowers continuing to open, as they will do well into early summer.

But there are new attractions. Golden, daisy-like flowers cover a great quarter-acre patch of the stream floodplain; scattered specimens of these golden ragworts are on the drier plateau above. In the rough talus near the main road there is celandine, an alien plant fond of limestone, and so attractive with its buttery, four-petalled blossoms and lush, pea-green leaves that it looks like a native. Garlic mustard, on the other hand, with its crowded growth and lean look, has all the marks of the weed it is. These aliens have gained ground in the disturbed portion of the limestone ledges.

On the plain behind the ledge there is a deeper forest of sugar maple, basswood, elm and black walnut. The bladdernuts are in prolific bloom now and swarming with many kinds of bees. The forest floor slopes gently off to the south. A bit downslope is a huge elm tree in the last throes of a losing battle against Dutch elm disease. A few branches on one side have started to leaf, but even these are now withering, and will be the last to try. In its dying is a new bounty; on the ground beneath the giant elm are troops of the strangest objects, mushrooms by their look, resembling sea sponges or old butternut husks, but more regularly pitted and ridged. These are the morels so prized by epicures. They are fond of this combination of dead elms and limey soils. Several species occur in our forests, always fruiting in spring, whereas most mushrooms fruit in late summer or fall.

While gathering our dinner of morels into a paper bag, we come across another mushroom on a rotting stump, a speckled shelf fungus called dryad's saddle, edible, but no prize when morels are available.

Beyond another patch of ragwort there seems to be another trail. This

Wild lily-of-the-valley
(*Mianthemum canadensis*)

Flowering dogwood (*Cornus florida*)

new path leads us into an area of small rock ridges with low vales between, almost like a range of tiny mountains. The moist soil here supports hemlock, and on the rocky outcrops, red cedar, these conifers supplying an element of shade so far unencountered in these woodlands. Here we find two prize flowers, well worth getting "lost" for an hour in uncharted territory. Both are yellow. The first, by its urn-shaped nectary and three twisted maroon sepals, is a wild orchid, the yellow lady-slipper. The other's yellow blossom is pendant and drapelike, the petals like twisted streamers, the leaves oblong and clasping the stem. It's the large-flowered bellwort, biggest and showiest of our three species. Nearby we also find in quantity the perfoliate bellwort, the middle-sized species named for its leaf which surrounds the stem.

As June draws closer, spring disappears from the valleys and lower slopes of the mountains, the leaves of trees having now shaded out the ground where flowering woodland herbs grow. Some of these are yellowing already; the toothworts especially look like plants after the first frost of autumn even now when a late spring frost is still a possibility. The brevity of spring coupled with its whirlwind succession of botanical events makes it the most compelling season for the field naturalist.

Some spring wildflowers occur over a wide elevational range which extends their period of blooming considerably. Among these are trilliums, Jack-in-the-pulpit, false hellebore and Canada, round-leaved and smooth

Apple (*Malus sylvestris*) blossoms

yellow violets. There are also a few spring bloomers which keep flowering well into summer, even to fall. Columbine and lyre-leaved rock cress do so, and the most enduring of all is harebell, the fragile, trailing bluebell of rocks and sands, which blooms from May through October.

As to when spring ends and summer begins, it depends upon the place. In the far north of the region and on the high mountains, the solstice may sometimes mark that natural point at which the burgeoning vegetation reaches maximum growth and settles into the business of summer's photosynthesizing and seed ripening. But for most of the region, spring is really over well before the middle of June. In the warmer valleys, full leafout may be reached well before the end of May.

The end of spring is no exact point in time, but sometimes I've experienced the change to summer as a sudden realization on a hot, sunny day when the leaves are no longer spring-tender, but toughening up for their defense against summer's insect marauders, and when the urge to go find some new flower before it blooms and vanishes has been quelled. The woods, beneath the exuberant greenery of the new leaves, is dark, only here and there sun-dappled. The bright splashes of color that were spring's greatest marvel are gone; even below the trees all is green. Only the most astute student of plants will now recognize the wood and rue anemones, the dwarf ginseng, the trilliums, bloodroot and lady-slippers. All have vanished into a carpet of greenery, where they must be sought out with the greatest care and effort, their distinct and colorful flags of identity now changed over to low-profile agents of reproduction. But it is a challenge now to learn these plants in their post-bloom aspect, as the commited botanist will want to learn to recognize a plant at any time of year.

But now another part of nature's world is seeking attention. As spring changes into summer, the open fields, marshes, bogs and fens, and dry barrens and brushlands begin to offer their blossoming elements for our inspection. Their season begins as that of the forest flowers wanes, and so next we will go to the places where the sun reigns all year, with no trees to cast shadows on plants that offer flowers to busy insect tongues and feet—and to human eyes and noses.

Cinnamon fern (*Osmunda cinnamomeum*) fiddlehead

EARLY SUMMER

IF spring is the season of woodland wildflowers and burgeoning leaves of shrubs and trees, then summer is the season of business as usual in the forest. By the time the leaves of all tree species have attained full size and toughened up against insect marauders, the giant explosion of forest wildflowers is over. Summer has come to the Northeast.

Summer does not come everywhere at once. It first arrives, as spring did, in the lowlands and in the southern parts of the region, and in those areas warmed by proximate waters—most especially the Hudson, Delaware, Connecticut and Housatonic valleys and the Ontario Lake Plain. Along the Atlantic coast, the ocean tends to delay all seasons because the water lags behind in temperature, cooling slowly in autumn and warming slowly in spring. Mountainous regions have shorter growing seasons, and so have late springs and early autumns. The highest mountains are treeless and have no spring as described in the previous section: the period of thawing is short, followed by a growing season typical of open environments at any elevation.

The period of peak activity in treeless plant communities corresponds closely to the period during which forest trees are in full leaf. This time is nature's summer. The date at which it begins can range from mid-May to late June depending on the climatic and environmental factors mentioned above. The attention of the nature lover is drawn away from the forest to the open meadows as summer begins. The power of the sun is available to grasses and herbs for the entire growing season, and as the season progresses, there follows a grand series of blossoming episodes running into early autumn. In the forest's shady season, only a few flowers appear, but these are quite interesting and worth seeking.

A field in early May is often little different from the same field in March. While the woods are blooming in a fury, the only sign of new growth in the fields are grasses, which commence growth early in the season in all habitats. This curious lack of plant activity in open lands can be understood with reference to the structure of the litter horizon, that layer of last year's plant remains which overlies the soil.

In the forest this litter consists of the leaves of trees which lie flat upon the ground. These leaves absorb heat and conduct it down to the soil

Bladder campion (*Silene cucubalus*)

Previous pages:
Field of day lilies (*Hemerocallis fulva*)

84

which quickly begins to thaw. The dark trunks of trees also serve as heat sinks in the woods. The litter of a field consists of the stalks of dead weeds and dried blades of grass lying thickly on the ground. This mass of old vegetable debris is loosely-packed; heat tends to get trapped in the upper part of it, the lower part remaining cold because the air is still and hardly circulates. Thus it takes much longer for the ground of a field to thaw out than it does the ground in a forest, given similar sunlight regimes.

As it is in the forest, in a field too, the shallowly rooted plants tend to begin growing and blooming before deeper-rooted, larger plants. There is a further logic to the rule of small things first in an open habitat, which is revealed as the summer progresses. It is a common observation that the weeds get higher and higher as the summer goes on. But the same weeds

Pale touch-me-not (*Impatiens pallida*)

Bullhead lily (*Nuphar variegatum*)

Wild geranium (*Geranium maculatum*)

do not just keep growing taller. Instead, a long progression of plants comes to bloom throughout the summer, those blooming later having the need to rise taller than those which have already bloomed, in order to reach the sunlight. The tallest flowering plants tend to bloom last, in the fall. There are exceptions to this rule; some plants, such as field milkwort and small skullcap, bloom hidden low among their taller neighbors.

One of the first flowers to bloom in weedy fields—even in hayfields or neglected lawns—is one of those which hides down among the old stems of the year before. This is blue-eyed grass, not really a grass, but a diminutive cousin of irises. The plant would surely go unnoticed save for its six-petalled blue-violet blossoms. A close examination of the plant shows the flat, interlocking leaves of the iris family.

The first wave of summer flowers begins in the lowlands in late May. An astute botanist could probably guess within a week the date of a photograph of an old field showing wild parsnip, yarrow, ox-eye daisy, cow vetch, beardtongue and bladder campion in bloom. These plants are so common in fields of the Northeast that they signal the start of summer almost everywhere. None of them are native plants; all arrived from Europe in the early years of settlement in the new world. They've taken over the pasturelands, roadsides and vacant lots of the open lands in populous neighborhoods, and later they spread from there to wilderness

Spotted touch-me-not
(*Impatiens capensis*)

areas by following highway corridors. With them came many kinds of grasses, some native, some alien, to form a patchwork prairie, a melting pot of plants akin to that of the people who settled the land.

These are among the plants closest to home, at least for most Northeasterners. They are the plants of farms and highways and neglected back lots of villages; even the cities have their share of these weeds. Closest to home of all are flowering plants which crop up in lawns, as they inevitably will, provided the lawns haven't received an overdose of weed killers. Such plants originally adapted to the grazing of animals; for centuries plants such as hawkweeds and pussytoes lived in the pastures of Europe, undaunted by grazing sheep and goats. Before that they had been tempered by the great grazers of the ice ages—the woolly rhinos and mammoths, wild camels, elk and deer and musk oxen. These persistent herbivores prepared them for the lawn mower.

Grasses also tolerate grazing (and mowing, of course), but the structural strategies of grasses and graze-tolerant herbs are different. Where grasses grow long, expendable leaves from a ground-level base, herbs such as hawkweeds and pussytoes produce basal rosettes, little wheels of leaves which lie flat against the ground below the level of mowers, and difficult for grazing animals to bite. The flower buds are elevated on long stalks, and are often eaten or mowed away if the timing is inopportune. But very shortly, within weeks or even days, new buds rise and the plants bloom again. Sooner or later some flowers are pollinated and set seed, propagating the species. These plants also propagate by sending out runners along the ground, permitting plant colonies slowly to shift position to better conditions.

The masters of this kind of ambulation are the cinquefoils. These creepers keep even their flowers close to the stem. They grow rapidly and linearly, extending a foot or more per growing season. The most common ones are dwarf, Canada and common cinquefoils, all trailing forms. Silvery, Norway and rough-fruited cinquefoils are upright and bushier. Three-toothed or alpine cinquefoil is a white-flowered species (the others bloom yellow) of mountain ridges and summits, northern sandplains and coastal cliffs. I found a small patch of it in a cow pasture on a Catskill

Chicory button (*Cichorium intybus*)

89

Sweet vernal grass (*Anthoxanthum odoratum*)

Bentgrass (*Agrostis*) with Eastern tailed blue butterfly (*Everes comyntas*)

Cow vetch (*Vicia cracca*)

mountainside, an uncharacteristic context. It appears to have seeded into that spot from a nearby colony on an open ledge, a more typical habitat for the plant. Nearly all cinquefoils grow in dry soil; exceptions are bushy cinquefoil, a plant of moist sands common on bay beaches and the Ontario Lake Plain; and shrubby cinquefoil, which grows in limey wetlands.

Low, creeping plants tend to be found where taller plants have a hard time growing. This may be due to the effects of herbivores or to poor soil. Grazing animals feed on fast-growing upright plants, especially grasses, allowing sunlight to reach the creepers, which largely escape grazing by growing so close to the ground. Poor soils support fewer plants, so there is room to stretch out. Some creepers root from their runners in pockets of better or deeper soil in a generally poor soil context. In deep, rich soils, ground creepers get shaded out by tall plants.

Other trailing plants have the habit of growing over tall, upright weeds, twining in the sun of the weeds' upper stalks. One of the most common of these viney herbs is cow vetch, an element of almost every hayfield and oldfield in the region. Its blue or purple blossoms, borne on a spike, and compound leaves with terminal tendrils mark it as a type of pea. There are native vetches in the Northeast but they are rare compared to cow vetch, and some are hard to distinguish from the more common alien.

Bindweeds are another group of annual vines or trailers. They look very much like their cultivated cousins the morning glories, bearing large, white or pink-and-white-striped flowers as they trail on for yards through grasses, weeds and small shrubs, or over fence rails or highway safety railings. As taller weeds rise above those which have seeded, a process that goes on throughout the summer, the bindweeds simply reach up and grab the higher plants as they grow. This is a highly efficient form of growth, as it eliminates the need to build stiff, strong supporting structures. A vine is free to be lightweight, though it must be tough enough not to be easily broken. More energy is available for leaf-building and blooming, and for rapid growth to great length. Vines need fewer nutrient and mineral resources, and most survive without taking these from plants on which they climb. An exception is dodder, which eventually breaks its connection to the soil, and feeds from a host plant, often jewelweed or purple loosestrife.

The forms of plants in any community are varied and serve to complement each other to avoid direct competition. The forms of flowers, too, follow such a rule and for similar ecological reasons. A field in June (or any time through September) is an excellent place to observe the many forms flowers assume. The bindweeds have their big, simple open bells; the milkweeds their globe of five-part starry blooms; jewelweed its curious golden urns; wild parsnip and wild carrot (queen anne's lace) their flat discs of tiny florets. The variety of forms is astounding. What's the reason?

In a complex community like a field of flowers, a rule of evolution is at work. After thousands or millions of years of coexistence, competition leads to specialization. This could be stated as the principle that it's easier to succeed by doing something different than by doing the same thing better than your competitors. Plants are dependent on insect pollinators, so they must attract these insects; they have to advertise. The bright colors and unusual forms of flowers often have to do with getting the attention of insects. Over the eons, different plants have specialized in attracting particular types or sizes of insects. Plants with large flowers attract larger insects. Some of these flowers have deep nectaries accessible only to long-tongued insects such as bumblebees, large butterflies and large moths. Other flowers are so small that only tiny flies and miniature wasps take an interest in them.

A different mix of plants will be found in open wetlands than in the drier fields and roadsides. One common type of open wetland is the small stream floodplain, which in its non-forested form is usually a moist meadow, grassy, weedy, brushy, or a combination of these types. One of the first flowers to bloom in wet meadows is the common blue flag, a wild iris smaller than most cultivated irises but no less beautiful. This plant often grows directly in muddy stream beds. Yellow iris, an alien species, is found in freshwater marshes along with native marsh plants such as angelica, sweet flag, cow parsnip and cat-tail. A rarer plant in this context is golden-club, which occurs in tidal marshes of the Hudson River above the salt front.

Square-stemmed monkey-flower
(*Mimulus ringens*)

Butter-and-eggs (*Linaria vulgaris*)

Musk mallow (*Malva moschata*)

Early summer is also the season in which truly aquatic plants bloom. Waterlilies are the most familiar of these, being quite spectacular in bloom, and having been cultivated as pond ornamentals for centuries. No cultivated waterlilies have gone wild, so any water lilies encountered in open marshes and woodland ponds are native species. Of these five, one is white and four are yellow. Less familiar aquatic plants are arrowheads, pickerelweed, water plantains, floating-hearts and bladderworts. The first three are plants of shallows and pond edges; the last two are found in open water. Bladderworts are especially interesting for their carnivorous habit. The leaves and stems lie in the water with the flowers rising on stalks above the surface. Underwater stems are dotted with little bladders which are spring traps for tiny insects and crustaceans. Carnivorous plants "eat" small animals to obtain minerals. Such plants are found in mineral-poor environments such as sphagnum bogs or, in the case of bladderworts, unrooted in pond water.

Probably the most fascinating wetlands are bogs and fens, for these contain not just carnivorous plants of several kinds but also many of the region's wild orchids and other plants not found in any other kind of environment. June is usually the month the bogs start blooming. Bogs take a long time to warm up, longer even than meadows.

Finding bogs is not easy. More often than not, bogs are hidden in wooded areas and you must just be lucky enough to stumble upon one during a walk in the woods. Looking for round bodies of water on topographic maps can narrow down the field somewhat, but often these features turn out to be rather ordinary ponds. Bogs with no open water center may not be marked at all.

The dominant plants in most bogs are sphagnum mosses. Some sphagnum mosses are green, while others are a gorgeous maroon. The colors are especially vivid after a rain. Different species of sphagnum can be found in wetter and drier parts of a bog.

Carnivorous plants are also frequent in bogs. The pitcher plant is a striking resident of many bogs throughout the Northeast, with its urn-like maroon leaves and a blossom so tough as to make it resemble in texture a plastic flower. The pitcher-shaped leaves are effective insect traps, being

Moss caps (*Mnium sp.*)

lined with recurved hairs which make a grip almost impossible to obtain. Insects drown in the water which gathers in the middle of the pitcher, where digestive enzymes and resident bacteria break their bodies down.

Sundews are small plants which trap insects on the sticky hairs of their leaves. They are found in bogs and on moist barren sands. The leaf shape is the best way to tell one species from another. Though small, sundews are weirdly beautiful plants, eye-catching as their globules of moisture glint brightly in the sun. They, too, are maroon, a common color among bog plants, perhaps due to their heavy tannin content. Sundews' white or pink flowers are borne on an upright, slowly uncurling spike.

The most magnificent bog-dwellers are the orchids. Though they are found in many other habitats, especially sedgy fens and limey swamps, in a bog they stand out regally because the other plants are so small and modest or dark in color. Orchids bloom from early summer through fall, but particular species bloom at various times throughout this period. June and July are especially good months to pursue orchids. Orchids assume two basic forms, one group having single, large flowers, the others bearing flowers in numbers along a spike. A few forms are borderline, such as the showy lady-slipper, our largest species, whose magnificent pink and white blossoms are borne two or three to a stalk. Some orchids are very rare, such as the ram's head and sparrow's egg lady-slippers, and the smaller whorled pogonia. An encounter with one of these is an event of a lifetime.

The greatest variety of wetland flowers will be found in mineral-rich wetlands or in those with a variety of associated wetland types. If limestone bedrock underlies the wetland, or serves as a source of dissolved nutrients and minerals by way of a feeder stream, a greater variety of plants will be able to live there. Waters of varying depth further enhance wetland diversity. It pays to explore every square yard of a wetland carefully, if not in one visit, then after a more cursory and fast-paced first visit. Some plants may hide low among others, or may be overlooked in favor of fancier attractions. These plants may turn out to be very striking later in the season, when they bloom or their foliage turns color. Finding them early and noting the stage of growth helps in planning subsequent visits to the site.

Helleborine (*Epipactus helleborine*)

Jewelweed (*Impatiens capensis*)

ʲ

Showy lady-slipper (*Cypripedium reginae*)

In contrast to oldfields, open wetlands seem less prone to takeover by alien species. If disturbed, however, by agricultural activities, damming, draining, siltation or vehicular traffic, alien plants such as purple loosestrife and adventive natives such as smartweeds and sticktights may gain hold and displace rare native plants. Visitors to fragile wetlands should be careful not to damage plants or overly disturb the soil. It is perhaps even a good precaution to clean one's boots before entering a fen or bog in order to wash off any lingering weed seeds!

There are some habitats which can be wet during part of the year and dry during another part of the season. Dense clays often form the subsoil in these places; water is only very slowly absorbed by this kind of soil, and so tends to flood the land instead of soaking into it and draining off through porous underlayers. In contrast to this tendency to flood, these habitats have an opposite tendency to dry out when rain is scarce or occurs in small doses which quickly evaporate. The wet-dry chronology in such places usually follows this pattern: in spring the lands flood, favoring early summer-blooming plants with wetland affinities; in late summer the land dries out, favoring more dry-loving plants. In addition to these plants, such lands may contain plants well-adapted to just such a flooding/drying out regime. These wet/dry lands tend to be rich in species because they accommodate diverse ecological needs, but this is tempered by the diversity-dampening hard clay soils of many wet/dry environments.

In the early part of the growing season, the wet season, swamp buttercup is often a dominant plant, dotting the early June greenery with myriad yellow splotches. Water hemlock, long-leaved chickweed, swamp candles, moneywort and a variety of sedges and grasses typical of wet ground can be found in these bimodal plant communities in early summer. Missing from the flora will be plants which require a constant water supply year-round, such as marsh St. Johnswort, the wetland orchids, and marsh plants such as angelica and sweet flag.

In dry habitats, early summer may be the most productive season because frequent precipitation is coupled with high temperature. Later, drought may severely inhibit growth and stimulate plants of drylands to resort to water conservation measures which may include the elimination

White beardtongue (*Penstemon digitalis*)

100

of exposed foliage, making them difficult or impossible to find later in the summer. Plants with xeric-adapted (tolerant of dryness) foliage may still be highly visible, but out of bloom.

Sedums are common plants of dry habitats. The cultivated varieties are well known as rock garden plants, and it is these that are most often encountered in wild places, having escaped from gardens. The native sedums are much harder to find. One of these, wild stonecrop, is not a dry-loving plant at all; it is an infrequent resident of floodplains, moist banks and rocks with springs supplying copious moisture. Sheep sorrel is another common plant of dry, poor soils, especially clays and shale crumble, which results from the weathering of shale bedrock exposures. Elevated clay banks often support dry-adapted grasses and such early blooming herbs as wild strawberry, bluets and silvery cinquefoil. Later in the season, other, taller plants come into bloom just as they do in the richer clays and silts of old fields and prairie-like meadows.

The driest habitats in the Northeast are bare rock exposures and sand plains. Large, level bedrock areas (pavement barrens) and sandplains with prominent pines are often called pine barrens. Some talus slopes are very dry and well-drained and should also be included in this category of plant communities as should elevated gravel plains and beach deposits.

One visible difference between these communities and wetter types is the spacing of the plants. In drylands plants are often spaced widely, almost as in the most extreme examples of this kind of community—deserts. On bare rock, this is often simply because rootholds are few, confined mostly to cracks in the rock or pits where soil can accumulate. In granular soils, nutrients are scarce, so plants must expand their root areas in order to collect sufficient water and food; hence they cannot be spaced as densely as in richer soils. These plants have evolved strategies to avoid crowding each other, which during a period of high stress (such as drought or severe winter cold), could result in the death of nearly all of the plants.

Sandplains are unusual environments, the most desert-like habitats in the Northeast. Though they receive adequate rainfall, water quickly drains off through the sandy substrate or sinks to the level of deep aquifers

Silvery cinquefoil (*Potentilla argentea*)

Polytrichum moss

(underground reservoirs of water-saturated sands, clays or rock). Sandplain plants are well-adapted to dry soils, having excellent water storage capacity or leaves which reduce evaporation by being very narrow or very tough.

In early summer the flowering herbs and grasses of sandplains are at their finest. Goat's-rue and blue lupine, both wild peas, are the most elegant and showy of sandplain flowers. Goat's-rue has globular clusters of pink and yellow blossoms; lupine's flowers are large, borne on spikes and blue to lavender in color. In New York and New Hampshire, the lupines of some sandplains support populations of the rare Karner blue butterfly.

The overall vegetational character of most sandplains ranges from prairie-like to shrubby to sparsely forested (pine barrens). Usually there is a great deal of open land or lightly shaded areas, excellent for sun-loving herbs. Starry false solomon's seal and great solomon's seal are early summer plants of thickets and other partly shady places. Few herbs grow in the shade of dense shrubs such as scrub oak and blueberries. One that does is wild indigo. These shrubs are remarkable for their dwarfed size and resistance to fire, a common occurrence in brushy sandplains.

Grasses such as bluestems, panic grasses, silver hairgrass, brome grasses, indian grass, sweet vernal grass, poverty grass and others, combine to form intermittent grasslands among the brushlands and forests of sandplains. In this prairie-like context may be found flowering plants such as pine-barrens toadflax, stiff sandwort, frostweeds and blunt-leaved milkweed, all early summer flowerers. Dryland sedges such as crested and hillside sedges may also mingle with the grasses and herbs.

Sandplains are home to spurges with their inconspicuous, oddly leaflike flowers. Eight spurges are recorded from the Albany Pine Bush, for instance, half of which are alien species, including the common cypress spurge of dry road banks. The four native species include the rare nodding and hairy spurges. Spurges' leafy floral bracts are often a slightly different color from the real leaves; the actual flowers are very small structures at the centers of the leafy rosettes.

Beaches are often similar to sandplains, especially back behind the shore where sands have drifted to form high dunes. Grasses often

Least hop clover (*Trifolium dubium*)

103

dominate these beachlands, even to the exclusion of herbs, shrubs and trees. Grasses are better able to survive the unpredictable drifting of the sands; if they are buried, they can grow up through the deep sands to find the air, or they may grow tremendously long runners which when exposed to the air or shallower sands, send up leaves to catch the sun. Where herbs grow on beaches, they are often similar to those of inland sandplains, sometimes the same species. Beach pea is similar to lupine and goat's-rue, and other wild peas such as vetchling and purple vetch are also fond of beaches. Wrinkled rose, one of our most beautiful wild roses, may form thickets or hedgelike barriers behind the sea beach on higher dunes. More wind-stressed beaches (and some inland sandplains) may support the ground-hugging shrubs false heather and golden heather, which produce numerous small yellow blossoms in early summer.

Moist sands along the Atlantic coast have yet other plants to offer the beachcombing botanist. Only protected back bays, estuaries and tidal shallows support plant communities of a brackish (slightly salt-loving) affinity. Among the prettiest flowers of the Northeast's salt marshes are the mallows, which include the seashore mallow and the marsh mallow with their big pink blossoms so much like crepe paper flowers. The major floral component of marshes is grass, especially cordgrasses (*Spartina*). Marsh grasses form uniform communities of superficially monotonous appearance (e.g. the "meadows" of urban northern New Jersey). Such places are difficult to explore; one can easily get lost in the jungle of grasses and reeds which tower a foot or more overhead. Fortunately, the most diverse and interesting plant communities in salt marshes are to be found along the edges (ecotones) of the marsh and adjoining ecosystems—forests, dryer brushlands or fields, or islands of higher ground within the marsh.

Some beachlands, especially the more northerly shores of the Atlantic, are elevated bluffs of rock, clay, or in at least one case, peat. These places would be drylands except for the ocean spray and frequent fogs which contribute abundant moisture. These high shorelines may support odd mixtures of species found in other contexts—bog and fen plants, beach flora, plants typical of rock ledges or pavement barrens, and even alpine

Musk mallow (*Malva moschata*)

and tundra species at unusually low elevations or far south of their normal ranges. A large list could be made of such plants, but it would surely include three-toothed cinquefoil and Drummond's rock cress (coastal rock ledges); cloudberry, bog laurel and dwarf birch (coastal peatlands); deer's hair, tufted hairgrass and mountain sandwort (granular acid soils).

A good number of isolated sites in the Northeast are treeless by virtue of elevation. The farther north and the higher the elevation, the cooler and harsher the climate. The highest mountains of New York and New England are even harsher places than the arctic; on Mt. Washington and Mt. Marcy, winds of over 200 mph have been recorded. Not only does this create a wind chill factor, but it has a dessicating effect upon the peaks' soils and plants.

Mountain summits, though having fewer plant species than lowlands, have more rarities. A first-time visitor to a high peak such as Katahdin, Washington or Marcy will find few familiar plants. One finds only the very hardiest common weeds, such as self-heal and fireweed. Dry oldfield species such as pearly everlasting and crinkled hairgrass turn up, and other odds and ends such as harebell and closed gentian. Many common arctic plants—too many to mention, really—were stranded on mountain summits as the glaciers retreated and the climate grew warmer. A few plants, such as alpine goldenrod and Boott's rattlesnake-root, are found on northeastern mountain summits above treeline and nowhere else.

High mountain summits are late to spark to life, locked in the grip of winter for an extra month or two beyond the winter of lowland and moderately elevated plant communities. When spring comes, it's summer—not just by the calendar, but in the way the ground is suddenly unlocked from the prison of ice and thrust into the freedom of growth and fecundity. Summer in the alpine zone is not hot and muggy, but cool, and in the highest places, still subject to frost at night in any month.

Plants here are tiny, dwarfed both by the harsh conditions and genetically, through thousands of years of evolutionary tempering. Trees of sorts are here—willows and birches—but they are not even of shrub status, being so tiny and slow-growing as to be natural bonsais, or more like ground covers. June or July finds in bloom charming dwarf shrubs

Heal-all (*Prunella vulgaris*)

105

Heal-all (*Prunella vulgaris*)

Canada lily (*Lilium canadense*)

such as alpine azalea and mountain heath, and herbs such as alpine cress, Hornemann's and alpine willow-herbs, and diapensia. Less conspicuous but more ubiquitous are alpine grasses and sedges, and a host of mosses and lichens more diverse and colorful than those found at lower elevations.

Although mountaintops are typically dry, on large, broad summits, hollow spots fill with water and bogs sometimes develop in these places. Here are found the tundra elements and many of the plants found in bogs and fens at lower elevations. In contrast to these alpine wetlands are areas of bare rock so hard and uninviting that only lichens will grow there.

The rarest alpine plants occur only at a few small sites or on only one or two mountain summits. Star-like saxifrage is known in the Northeast only from Mt. Katahdin in Maine. Dwarf alpine cinquefoil is found only on Mt. Washington and a few disjunct summits of the Franconia range in New Hampshire. Alpine speedwell is confined to alpine streams of two mountains (Katahdin and Washington). These two mountains are the richest in alpine plants, Washington being the highest point in the Northeast (6288 ft.) and Katahdin the northernmost mountain.

Although open habitats are the most prolific in flowers during early summer, woodlands are not without interest, and to neglect them entirely would be to miss considerable beauty. A number of spring-blooming herbs continue to bloom into early summer and even longer. Canada and

Hedge bindweed (*Convolvulus sepium*)

smooth yellow violets produce more flowers over a longer season than any other violets. On lower slopes of mountains in deep rich soils, these flowers may form great beds which grow higher and more full of flowers as the season progresses, reaching a peak after the tree leaves have expanded.

Openings in the forest canopy let in enough sunlight to permit herbaceous plants to photosynthesize and bloom after the leaves have expanded. Certain kinds of places create openings in the shade which remain for many years, and these, rather than short-term openings such as blowdowns, are the best places to look for flowering plants in early summer. Streambeds may be wide enough to provide breaks in the canopy, and they also supply water. Jewelweeds are common summer-blooming plants of streamsides and seeps. Their deep nectaries attract hummingbirds and butterflies. Climbing fumitory, a viney relative of squirrel corn and dutchman's breeches, grows in the gravel of rocky streambeds and on coarse talus where trees are widely spaced. Monks-hood, one of the region's rarest plants, grows only in eastern New York's Catskill Mountains along steeply sloped streams, on spring seeps or near waterfalls, or on steep talus slopes with cold springs.

Some mountain slope plants are tolerant of shade, such as the white-flowered white snakeroot, a plant so common in some woodlands as to be considered a native weed. Another plant of rich talus which continues to bloom through the summer is herb-robert, a wild geranium. Dry talus of shale or ledges of sandstone may support an occasional corydalis plant with its peculiar fish-shaped blossoms. Pale corydalis, with pink and yellow flowers, is the most common. Golden corydalis, a plant of pavement barrens and sandplains, is found infrequently on open ledges in woodlands or in old quarries.

While wandering the early summer woodlands in search of flowers, it pays to look up from the ground from time to time. Some shrubs and trees bloom at or soon after the time their leaves are mature. Several large heaths bloom in June or July. The most familiar is mountain laurel, a medium-sized shrub of acid woods. Its flowers (and those of its near relatives, sheep laurel and bog laurel) are worth examining carefully. The flower buds, just before opening, look like tiny patty pan squashes. In the

Heal-all (*Prunella vulgaris*) leaf

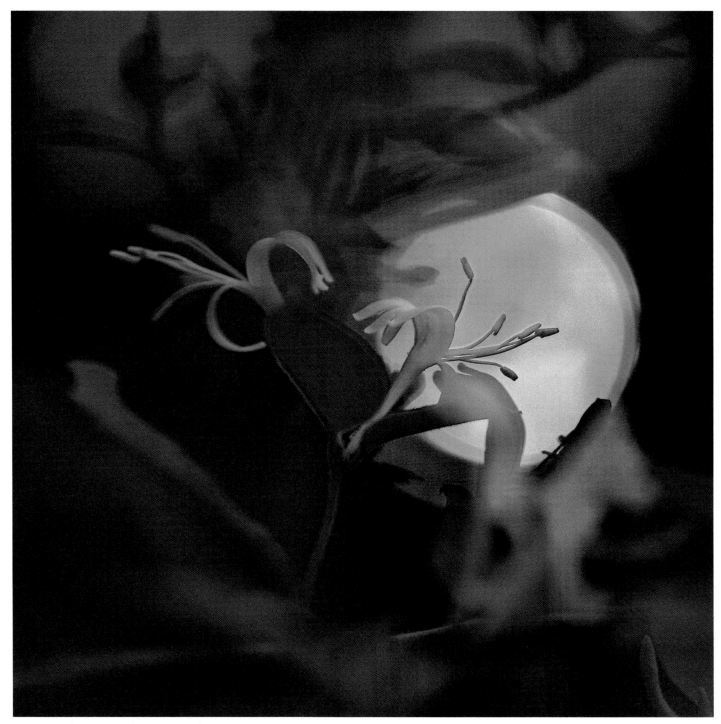

Japanese honeysuckle against the setting sun (*Lonicera japonica*)

Purple nightshade (*Solanum dulcamara*)
Wild strawberry (*Fragaria virginiana*) leaf with dew

open flowers, the stamens seem to arch back against the fused petals as if holding the flower open in a most unusual design.

Our most spectacular heath is the great rhododendron, an inhabitant of peaty or sandy swamp forests, often forming dense thickets akin to the "hells" of the southern Appalachians formed by this plant's cousin, the catawba rhododendron. The great rhododendron blooms in June or July, depending on latitude and elevation, and can reach the status of a small tree, some specimens being over 30 feet high.

In moist ravines ninebark may be a common flowering shrub. A much rarer and more spectacular ravine shrub is wild hydrangea. Flowering shrubs of the genus Viburnum are common elements of many deciduous forest understories and occur also in open brushlands. Viburnums have flat clusters (racemes) of white or creamy flowers. The most spectacular

Pasture rose (*Rosa carolina*)

species is hobblebush, a shrub of mountains and the northern parts of the region. Some of the flowers around the edge of the cluster are greatly enlarged in this species.

A few trees produce large, showy and sometimes aromatic flowers. Catalpa, known for its cigar-shaped pods, produces ruffled bunches of snapdragon-like blossoms in June and July. Catalpa is a native tree, but its natural range is confined to the lower Mississippi Valley. It has been so widely planted as an ornamental that it is now found throughout the Northeast and Midwest, but it has never "gone wild" to become a common element of forests.

Tuliptree, one of the region's most spectacular hardwoods, produces huge yellow-and-orange tulip-like flowers . Unfortunately, mature tuliptrees are not only tall (often over 100 feet), but as they grow, they lose their lower branches; a big tuliptree may have no branches for the first forty or fifty feet of trunk! A good look at the flowers can only be obtained by finding a ledge that looks out across the tops of the trees or by finding fallen flowers on the ground.

Locusts are more accessible. Members of the pea family (or, as some authors prefer, a related family of woodier pea-like plants), locusts produce flowers prolifically, and they are among the most beautiful and sweet-smelling of tree blossoms. If a grove of locusts is in bloom, it can often be found by literally following one's nose! Locusts are not common in the wild, though they are widely planted. Wild groves usually occur on sandy or gravelly soils. Locusts have invaded the edges of some sandplain communities in the Northeast, after disturbance or when fires are suppressed, along with poplars and other less fire-resistant species which move in to displace the fire-hardy pitch pines and scrub oaks.

By the peak heat of mid-July, a hiatus of growth and blossomings sets in, a sort of laziness of nature akin to that of people in midsummer. This slowdown presages the long decline which leads to autumn's colored leaves and tall bouquets of late asters and goldenrods. The very first of these two dominant groups of late summer flowers may be said to mark the transition point between early summer's youthful exuberance and the more staid and mature floral events of late summer.

Everlasting pea (*Lathyrus latifolius*)

LATE SUMMER

SUMMER crests and starts to decline toward fall with the shortening of the days after the summer solstice. Nature, as always, lags several weeks behind the celestial calendar. The peak temperatures of summer come in July for most of the Northeast, and August can be a hot month in the southern part of the region, especially along the Atlantic coast. The longer the growing season, the less definable the midpoint of summer is, and the more arbitrarily it must be chosen.

A valid benchmark for the beginning of summer's second phase is the sudden rise in the number of insect voices in field and forest. Grasshoppers of all kinds sing by day, along with the louder and stouter cicadas. Night brings the chorus of the grasshoppers' close cousins, the katydids and tree crickets.

In the world of plants, no big change marks the mid-point of summer. It sneaks up gradually as the early summer-blooming plants set seed and dry out giving way to a wave of late summer wildflowers which continue blooming into early fall and in some cases until frost or beyond. Late summer is also the season of mushrooms, which may appear suddenly in

Painted bolete (*Suillus pictus*)

Previous pages:
Meadow with goldenrods
(*Solidago spp.*)

huge numbers after rains. The first mushroom explosion of the year may be said to usher in the mid-life of the growing season, but in this mushrooms are not reliable; they appear some years and are scarce in others. In good years, forest mushrooms put on a spectacular show of diverse colors and shapes.

From mid-July until frost, no type of habitat outshines any other in terms of interesting and colorful plant expressions. Fields, sandplains, rock barrens and wetlands which held interest in early summer continue to change with the advancing season, as new plants come into bloom. Many of the plants that bloomed earlier set seed and die, while others continue to produce blossoms as the older ones progress to seed. The more slow-growing plants rise above the early summer flowers to open their buds and present fresh flowers to insect pollinators which, in late summer, reach their highest numbers.

As summer progresses, a weedy field may take on the structure of a forest, with a canopy of taller, tree-like weeds and an understory of smaller ones. Some of these lower plants are the dormant forms of earlier bloomers, but not all. There are a few herbs which seem to require the partial shade of taller weeds, but these species are not found in forests, probably because they could not survive being buried by leaves. Many puzzles present themselves while one explores a field through the growing season. Sometimes the answers need only to be awaited; sometimes the mystery remains.

I first noticed the layered structure of some fields while Anita was photographing flowers, sometimes a lengthy process. This allowed me to engage in some very patient procedures of exploration, literally getting down with the plants to ground level. To my surprise I found that not only were there interesting things about the lower parts of the more obvious plants in the field, but there were at least two kinds of plants so tiny that they'd never be noticed by simply walking through the field. One was a little daisy-like yellow flower, dwarf dandelion, a native species (the common dandelion is a European plant.) The other was an even tinier plant, readily recognizable as a milkwort or a smartweed. As it turned out, the plant was a milkwort, possibly Nuttal's milkwort: a

Columbine (*Aquilegia canadensis*) seedpod.

117

Bell's honeysuckle (*Lonicera x belli*) berries

Rabbit's-foot clover (*Trifolium arvense*)

precise identification was beyond my expertise. Looking back, I wish I'd kept a specimen to send to a plant taxonomist. I know now the importance of collecting plants for later identification by an expert. Anyone can find a rarity. The place I found that milkwort is gone now, lost when an industrial firm developed the site. I learned something of the complexity of a community of plants, and I wonder if more attention to the details of what I found would have saved the place. Was my milkwort a rare species? I'll never know.

Milkworts are no doubt unfamiliar to most people, even those who take an interest in nature. The organic world is so diverse that some groups of plants are still little understood and offer opportunities for investigation for both professional and amateur botanists. Even in the humble wilds around home, there are surprises waiting. One such surprise was the cardinal flower field.

Of all the reds in nature, that of the cardinal flower is by far the most intense, virtually a day-glo red, redder than the bird from which the flower gets its name. Cardinal flower is a plant of moist soils. I knew it from streambeds where it grows in the gravels and silts of banks and small islands and gravel bars in the stream itself. I had also found the plant along slow, muddy streams in thin woodlands and once in a wet roadside ditch beside a culvert. I had never found more than a few plants in one place.

Then one August we found a whole field of cardinal flowers—hundreds of big, robust, beautiful plants in a wet meadow fed by a sluggish stream, a painter's daydream come true. Of course there were other plants in this field—many species, including the aggressive invader, purple loosestrife. I remember puzzling over the sickly look of the loosestrife, stunted plants with leaves going to fall color months before their time.

In subsequent years the loosestrife started looking better, apparently getting healthier, and the cardinal flowers declined precipitously to perhaps a tenth of their earlier abundance. Conditions had changed, but what conditions and why I cannot say. The makeup of our plant communities is constantly changing for many reasons. It's evident especially in the species composition of the roadside plant community. From

Red bolete (*Boletus rubellus*)

year to year different plants are especially prominent; one year it may be white sweet clover, another birdfoot trefoil, yet another viper's bugloss or some other weed.

Certain plants more than others signal the decline of summer. Goldenrods are probably the most familiar of these. Less familiar ones might be Joe-Pye-weeds, thistles and asters. Goldenrods stand out because there are so many species, and because they literally paint the landscape golden in late summer as more and more goldenrod species come into bloom. There are many flowers in the fields at this time, but none so ubiquitous and so obvious from a distance. Nearly everyone knows goldenrod generically, but try to learn the individual species sometime. Only the most patient and determined will persist and learn to tell one kind from another; most people will find the genus hopelessly frustrating and leave identification to the professionals. When I first started learning wildflowers I dug into the goldenrod genus vigorously, learned the easy ones and after that left them alone, taking notice of them only as a sign of the fall of summer. Now I've returned to them.

Every field has its goldenrods, but there are other things to find and treasure such as the golden, wiry dodder that strangles the purple loosestrife, or the orange butterflyweed, a milkweed of limey soils that lives up to its name in its irresistibility to showy butterflies.

A place may beckon time after time over many seasons, but the traveler never stops, too much in a rush to a predetermined destination. After too much of this missing out, I decided to make these places the destinations of journeys, and this resolve has been amply rewarded. At one of these field stops there was a plant of a striking appearance, a super plant from the look of it—thick, fuzzy stem, blunt, leathery leaves; tall stalk with floral buds unfurling like something familiar. What was it that this plant suggested? A giant forget-me-not or comfrey or hound's-tongue, something in the family Scrophulariaceae, or as botanists call them, Scrophs. I would have bet on this plant proving to be a Scroph when it came into flower.

Two weeks later the plant had grown just a little beyond its progress when first discovered. Two weeks after that it still hadn't opened a bud, but now the strange tendrils of florets were greatly extended and still

Spotted knapweed (*Centaurea maculata*)

121

Shadbush (*Amelanchier*) berry

Cardinal flower (*Lobelia cardinalis*)

unraveling, more Scroph-like than ever. But when was it going to bloom?

Another week went by and it seemed the right time to return. Maybe the plant still wouldn't be in bloom. I just didn't want to miss it. I'd looked at every Scroph in the book trying to guess which one it would turn out to be. None seemed quite right. When we reached the field, the closest plant still wasn't quite in bloom. But maybe another one was, somewhere out farther in the field. The goldenrods certainly were blooming abundantly; and one kind stood out particularly fluffy and deeper gold than the others; it might be worth a closer look.

As I approached one of these big, showy goldenrods, I realized with a shock that the mystery plant had indeed bloomed—it was this big goldenrod. A goldenrod was the last thing I expected. It hadn't looked like one until it bloomed. Turning to the pages of goldenrod in Peterson's Field Guide I found it readily—stiff goldenrod, a prairie species. It turned out to be highly ranked on the New York Natural Heritage Program's list of rare plants, and here was a hundred-acre field where it was not uncommon!

There were milkworts in that field, too—not white-flowered ones but ones with magenta blossoms. They were field milkwort, a common species, and like the others, just a few inches tall and nestled way down among the lower leaves of taller plants, down where a person would have to hunch down to see them.

One curious thing about many weeds is that they can't be swayed from their mandate of reproduction by mowing; even herbicides can't kill the rootstocks of many common weeds; chemicals usually act as a selective agent, leaving the most resistant species such as spotted knapweed, bouncing bet and a number of grasses. When weeds are mowed down, they simply grow back, sometimes smaller than they might have been otherwise, and of course, tardy in their seasonal appearance. The blooming of such plants as queen anne's lace, yellow sweet clover, wild parsnip and common milkweed in late summer or early fall is nearly always the result of early summer mowing. Purple loosestrife responds vigorously to all forms of physical abuse, as does common ragweed.

A related phenomenon is the growth from apparently dead plants of

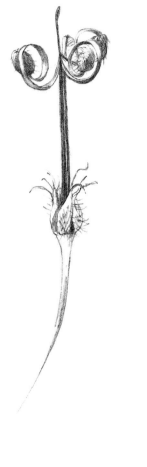

Wild geranium (*Geranium maculatum*) seedpod.

new green branches and new flowers very late in the growing season. Sweet clovers and certain mustards such as garlic mustard often come back from the dead in this way. Such peculiar behavior warns the botanist that many plants will occasionally be found in bloom at the "wrong" time of year.

If the goldenrods usher in the decline of summer, asters make it official. The wave of asters, a pointillistic display of whites, blues and purples, peaks in August or September. In the northern part of the region, some asters may begin blooming earlier, since the growing season is compressed in time. Both asters and goldenrods are primarily flowers of open fields, and most prefer dry to moderately moist soils. Wetlands have a good share of asters, but contain few goldenrods; rough-leaved, swamp and bog goldenrods are three. Open woodlands and forest edges have a number of both, species which prefer partial shade. The asters are a group as complex and difficult as the goldenrods, but several species are easy to recognize.

The flat-topped white aster's common name describes it perfectly and once recognized, this common aster can be readily spotted along road banks while driving. New York aster and New England aster are showy, purple to violet species common in wet meadows. Small white aster and calico aster often grow in country yards and gardens along with several common goldenrods. Other species must be sought in more exotic places.

Pine barrens and other very dry habitats are the haunts of narrow-leaved white-topped aster, eastern silvery aster, pine barren goldenrod and downy goldenrod. Wandlike goldenrod is the most slender species, occurring in moist parts of sandplains in the southern part of the Northeast, especially the New Jersey pine barrens. There's an alpine goldenrod that lives only on the highest mountains of New England and New York. The leafy-bracted aster, known from the mountains of Quebec, has not been found in mountains south of Canada except in the western United States, so the Northeast has no alpine aster. Several asters are found in mountain slope woodlands and on subalpine summits, and one species, serpentine aster, is restricted to the serpentine (a type of metal-rich rock) barrens of southeastern Pennsylvania and other parts of the Appalachians.

Groundnut (*Apios americana*) flowers

125

Ragged fringed orchis (*Platanthera lacera*)   Coral mushroom (*Clavicorona pyxidata*)

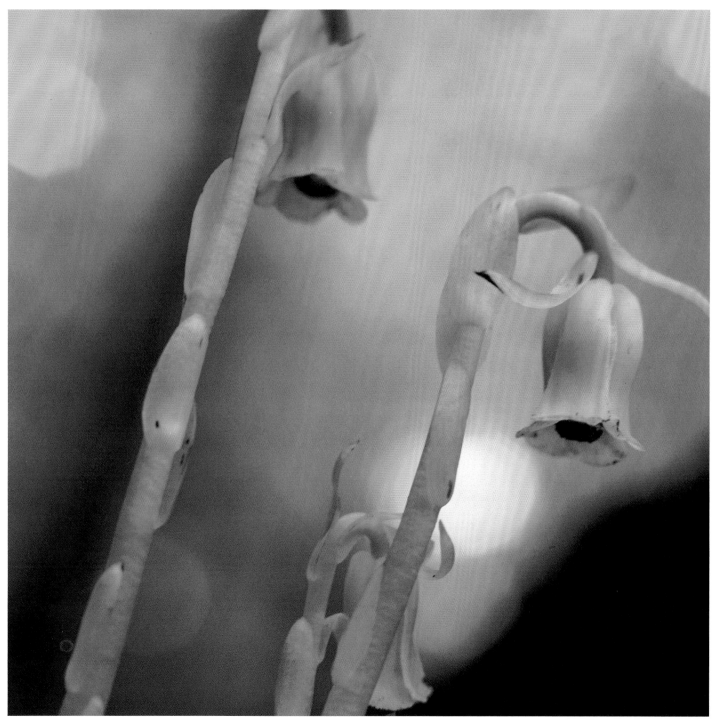

Indian pipes (*Monotropa uniflora*)

Cardinal flower (*Lobelia cardinalis*)

Many asters have a coastal affinity. These include wetland species such as low rough aster and the perennial and annual salt marsh asters; the latter is found (or was) at Onondaga Lake as well as in coastal salt marshes. Other coastal species are found in dry, sandy beach habitats, and may be found on old sandplains with species more typical of pine barrens. These include low, showy aster, Hervey's aster and eastern silvery aster.

Asters, because they are so diverse and reside in such a wide variety of habitats, are among the best cogeneric flowers to study for structural adaptations to environmental conditions. This is most apparent in the form of the leaves, and particularly in regard to available sunlight. Asters living in shaded places have very broad leaves; the basal leaves are especially big and wide to catch the sun through the spring and early summer as the plants store energy for the process of blooming and setting seed. Asters of open fields have narrower leaves, and some asters of very dry soils have almost needlelike leaves (e.g. the stiff aster of pavement barrens and sandplains). Salt marsh asters have long, grass-like leaves. Narrow leaves reduce water loss, an important consideration in dry soils or salt water, where moisture loss would concentrate the salt in the plants' tissues.

Late summer is when taller herbs come into bloom; the tallest herbs bloom at the end of the growing season. Among these are the Joe-Pye-weeds of wet meadows and brushy wetland edges. These plants produce great pom-pons of dull pink flowers, invariably attended by bevies of bees, butterflies, beetles and wasps in the day time, and at night by other kinds of beetles and by moths, the butterflies' nocturnal counterparts. These pollinators in turn attract predators such as spiders and assassin bugs which are often colored and patterned so as to blend in to the flowers. A patch of Joe-Pye-weed is a very busy place.

Even taller are the wild sunflowers. Joe-Pye-weeds may tower slightly above one's head, but one species of wild sunflower, the giant sunflower, may attain a height of over ten feet. This height is rivaled by several wild lettuces, but lettuces produce their tiny flowers at night, and their stalks are so poorly-leaved and pole-like that they fail to attract much attention.

Sunflowers, on the other hand, lure in many creatures with their huge, happy blossoms.

I have found sunflowers to be the most reliable haunts of the monarch butterflies on their late summer migration south; they always seem to linger long and lazily over a patch of sunflowers. These plants clone, producing new stalks from underground runners. By some mechanism, probably by "poisoning" the soil for other plants, sunflowers are able to occupy a patch of ground to the near exclusion of other species, forming a dense grove of plants almost like a garden planting. This is quite different from the more usual arrangement in nature of a mixed complex of many species.

The woodlands that provided the main floral attractions of early spring have a minor second blooming in late summer. From July to frost (September to November depending on climate) woodland plants come into bloom; some for a brief time only, others throughout the late summer. Among these are some that do not look at all like green plants, and functionally they are not. These are pale, ghostly things such as indian pipes and pinesap and coralroots. Taxonomically, they are "green plants," being closely related to wintergreen, and in the case of coralroots, orchids. But they have evolved to tap the resources of other plants, stealing nutrients from their roots. Having no need to produce chlorophyll for photosynthesis, it has disappeared from their leaves, which have atrophied to the status of tiny bracts.

A few summer-blooming woodland flowers are both parasitic (living off other plants) and photosynthetic. These include the brilliant yellow-blossomed false foxgloves and their tiny cousins the cow-wheats, members of the Scrophulariaceae, a family which includes our cultivated snapdragons and flowers of wet meadows such as turtlehead and obedient-plant, so named for its strange habit of staying in position when bent rather than twisting back to its original orientation.

Several summer orchids are found in wooded wetlands or in open wetlands deep in the woods. The most spectacular of these is the showy lady-slipper of partly shaded moist peatlands—peaty swamps, bog margins and brushy fens. Its huge pink-flushed white blossoms are among the most

Calocera mushroom

Giant sunflower (*Helianthus giganteus*)

Beechdrops (*Epifagus virginiana*)

spectacular sights in the cool woodlands of the northeast. It is an uncommon plant and those who know where it grows are guarded about giving out the lady-slipper's whereabouts. Even rarer are the small white lady-slipper and the ram's head lady-slipper, found only in a few fens of the region.

More common are the multi-flowered orchids of the genus *Platanthera*. These plants do not have big, showy flowers, but they are beautiful when viewed at close range. There are over a dozen species in the Northeast. The range of flower colors is wide—some are white, two are purple, one (very rare) is orange-yellow, and a few are green. These orchids bloom from July into early September. In September at summer's end, the ladies'-tresses, orchids of the genus *Spiranthes*, bloom. All are white-flowered, the blossoms borne on a tall spire in a spiral pattern around it. Two pink orchids also bloom in late summer—the grass pink of peaty swamps and the nodding pogonia of humus-rich cool woods, also charmingly called "three-birds" because it usually has three flowers per plant.

Lesser flowers of the woods of late summer are the pyrolas and wintergreens, all with small, white flowers and all fond of acid woodlands typified by the presence of oaks, pines and hemlock. Here too may be found the rattlesnake-plantains, the least orchid-like of all the members of the orchid family. Their white-reticulated leaves are more attractive than their dull greenish flowers.

Notable as well are some late-summer peas. Tick-trefoils are woodland plants with small, widely-spaced, but very bright lavender or violet pea-like blossoms. Bush clovers are stiff-stemmed, tough-looking clovers with typically creamy or yellowish blooms. Neither tick-trefoils nor bush clovers are especially eye-catching, but they are interesting as examples of how a plant may diverge in form from more familiar relatives yet still hold a family resemblance.

More than flowers, mushrooms dominate the woods of late summer, and some crop up in other contexts—pastures, lawns, wetlands, sand plains, even inside buildings. In recent years the idea that mushrooms are a form of plant life has been questioned; now most systematists assign the fungi to a kingdom of their own, equal to the plant and animal kingdoms.

Mycena mushrooms

Mushrooms are, in a sense, the fruit of the fungus; the working organism is something else, a network of fibers usually hidden underground or beneath the bark of a rotting tree. This fibrous complex is called the mycelium. Although more is now known about the functions of the mycelium than in the early years of the great mycologists Peck and McIlvaine, its life and functions remain mysterious. What is known is quite remarkable. Previously, fungi were thought of as rotters, plants which fed upon the bodies of dead plants or which killed living ones. While it is true that many fungi behave this way, most do not.

By far the most interesting lifestyle is that of the mycorrhizal fungus. "Myco" means fungus and "rhyz" is a Greek word for "root," simply enough. Plants, especially trees and shrubs, being locked in place, cannot go wandering about as animals do looking for things to eat. Organic nutrients are replenished rapidly, but minerals in the soil are slower to be released. One role of the fungus is to supply minerals to the roots of the

Indian pipes (*Monotropa uniflora*)

133

Turtlehead (*Chelone glabra*)

Caesar's mushroom (*Amanita caesarea*)

trees. Threads of fungus have been measured by radioactive tracing and found to be hundreds of miles in length! This may not be typical, considering the many barriers to such prodigious extension (often barriers of human invention). Still, it illustrates the mysterious power and importance of fungi in the lives of green plants, and hence our own. Except for aquatic algae, practically all green plants are dependent upon one or more mycorrhyzal fungi for their health if not their very existence.

After long association, plants and fungi have developed different tissue chemistries. While plants are mostly cellulose and carbohydrates, fungal tissue is closer to that of animals, rich in protein and mineral salts. In simplified terms, on a cellular level plants and fungi tend to cancel each other out; fungal-derived medicines (such as penicillin) kill bacteria and bacterial agents behave as fungicides (also virucides in some cases).

To see mycelia, turn over any log when the woods are moist in summer, or peel some bark off a rotting log. That webby stuff is the mycelium. Sometimes it's quite colorful, yellow, orange or blue, but more typically it's white. A few fungi such as the honey mushroom have tough, black mycelial fibers. Imagine then the whole soil mantle of the woods and fields, yards and gardens infused everywhere with the mycelial networks of hundreds, perhaps thousands, of species of fungi.

What we see and what we get are the fruit of the webs, the mushrooms brought on by wet weather in late summer and early fall. This period, from July until hard frost, constitutes a season, for mushroom lovers at least. It is not perfectly known why most mushroom species fruit in late summer and autumn. Cooler, moister weather may be an influence. So may the slowdown in the growth of woody plants, which are intimately tied to their fungal partners. As plant growth declines, perhaps the plants demand less from and release more to the fungi, which then may divert their energy to producing the fruiting bodies we call mushrooms. Whatever the reason, late summer in the forest is sometimes a time of such prolific fruiting of mushrooms that the ground may be almost swarming with mushrooms of dozens of species.

As any mycophile can tell you, mushroom hunting is one of the greatest adventures in nature. These fruits of the forest floor can be

Honey mushroom (*Armillaria mellea*)

136

appreciated in many ways. For sheer beauty and variety of form, they rival the wildflowers. Whereas many stretches of forest floor are devoid of flowering herbs, none is devoid of fungi. Though mushrooms appear only under the right conditions, and their abundance may fluctuate wildly from year to year, the mycelia are always there, ready to make mushrooms.

A good mushroom year is a great blessing, a time of treasures beyond measure. One of the best was 1979, and we happened to be situated in a fungi-rich forest on the west slope of Mt. Tobias in the Catskills. It's a woods with probably as many tree species as anywhere in those mountains, a place where northern and southern species intermingle, a forest of white pine, hemlock, beech, sugar, red and striped maples, red, white and chestnut oaks, shagbark hickory, hop- and American hornbeams, tuliptree, tupelo, yellow and black birches, basswood, sassafras and even the doomed shoots of American chestnut, ever suppressed by an introduced parasitic fungus which reduced this monarch of the American woodlands to a sickly shrub.

In August, after strong rains, the pageant commenced. First came the chanterelles, Russulas and Lactarii in shades of orange, red and buff. Soon followed the ghostly white Amanitas, the deadliest of all mushrooms, along with their relatives the fly mushroom, citron Amanita, panther cap and fly agaric. For the first time ever we found the edible Caesar's Amanita, a gorgeous scarlet and yellow mushroom, large and stately, but we didn't eat it—Amanitas are not to be trusted. Years later we discovered that American Caesar's mushroom is probably not the same species as the European "food of the gods," and that what resembles that legendary edible in our woods may be several related species whose edibility is questionable.

Mushrooms don't have to be eaten to be enjoyed. The very artsiness of these fabulous fruits make them worth hours of pleasure gazing, especially when the woods are transformed into a fungal sculpture gallery as they were in that summer. I think my favorites will always be the boletes, mushrooms of the genus *Boletus* and related genera, characterized by a typical mushroom shape (stem and cap) but having pores (many tiny holes, the ends of long tubes) rather than gills, through which the spores

Hedge bindweed (*Convolvulus sepium*) seed pod

Hebeloma crustuliniforme mushrooms

Hygrophorus nitidus mushrooms

are dispersed. All told, I listed 40 species of boletes for the Catskill woodlands near our home. These came in a great variety of color, form and size. Many were of reddish shades. The most abundant of these red boletes was a maroonish species of moderate size—*Boletus bicolor* or *Boletus rubellus* depending on which book you consult. I have no doubt that it has several other names; there is great confusion still in the taxonomy of fungi, with families and genera continually being revised and new species being named. But our *bicolor* or *rubellus* proved a pleasure to the eyes and to the palate.

How could we be sure this mushroom was edible when the experts were still disputing its pedigree even after examination of its microscopic spores and chemical tests on its tissues? Simply because the boletes contain very few poisonous species, and these are easily recognized. The general rule is to steer clear of boletes with reddish pores (the pores lie beneath the cap of the mushroom) and to be perfectly sure of the identification of any whose flesh ("context" in the mycologist's vernacular) stains blue when bruised. Though *bicolor* stains blue, it does so slowly, and no poisonous species resemble it.

One exciting result of a mushroom boom is that the rarer species seem to pop up with reasonable frequency while the common ones are simply superabundant. The chances of finding something you've never seen are greatly improved. Among the boletes we found a few rarities including the bizarre Frost's boletus and the luxuriant black velvet bolete whose surface is exactly like black velvet, more like an expensive toy than a mushroom. It's a decent edible, too. Under the low branches of hemlocks we found gigantic specimens (a foot across!) of the bitter bolete, a reddish buff relative of the black velvet. One would have made a meal in itself if it had been less bitter.

Prized for centuries as one of the most sublime of edible fungi is the stout cep or steinpilz, the mushroom whose latin name, *Boletus edulis*, bespeaks all too modestly its epicurean worth. In the case of this mushroom, the European and American versions are gastronomically the same. Often cropping up in groups, it seems to form mycorrhizal partnerships with both evergreen and deciduous trees.

Black chanterelle/trumpet-of-death
(*Craterellus fallax*)

I have most frequently found edible boletes on the outwash plains of small woodland streams or on forested terraces of the lower slopes of mountains, usually in association with hardwoods such as white ash, hop-hornbeam, oaks and hickories. In the west this mushroom is often associated with pines. The edible boletus is recognized by the reticulum (network of minute ridges) prominent at the top of the stem and often confluent with the pore layer. This netting pattern is light in color and raised above the surface of the stem, which may be darker or of the same color as the reticulum. The stem of the bitter boletus is darkly webbed. The cap of the edible boletus varies in color from nearly white through buff to pink and similar but darker shades. The cap is sometimes curiously wrinkled.

The boletus-hunting person, however, has competition for these mushrooms, creatures which get up earlier than any person could ever hope to. Most edible boleti are found to be riddled with tiny tunnels made by little white larvae of flies and beetles. These arthropod mycophiles are no less the connoisseurs than the most ardent mycologist. They go straight for the top-quality mushrooms, the ceps, and when the worms are fast and hungry, it's nearly impossible to find a decent mushroom. Even little buttons, tender infant mushrooms, will be tunneled mercilessly, and big ones may collapse to rubble before their growth is complete, so riddled are they with baby bugs.

It's a lucky boletus hunter who finds a clean cap. The best bet is to find the mushrooms in unusual situations where insects are scarce. A friend of ours once found dozens of *edulis* around an ash tree on a lawn, free of larvae. To his good fortune, the owner of the lawn was not a mycophagous sort, and was only too glad to let him take all he could cart away.

When we think of a mushroom, we think of a stem (stipe) and a cap (pileus), but mushrooms assume many other forms: fingers, antlers, coral-like shapes, spheres, shelves on stumps, etc. We once found a club mushroom shaped like a duck's head. One form of fungus is fancifully—and aptly—named dead man's fingers. Another is called tree ears. Puffballs are another offbeat form familiar to most nature-lovers. All these are as much mushrooms as agarics or boletes.

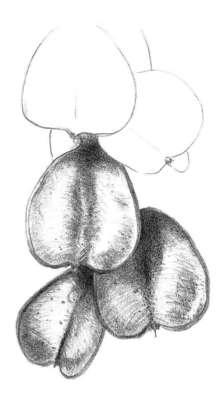

Wild yam (*Dioscorea villosa*) seedpods

141

Tricholoma mushroom

Groundnut (*Apios americana*)

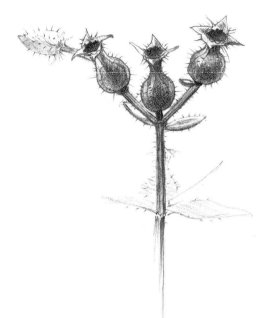

After eating many kinds of delicious mushrooms, I still find that mushrooms are even more impressive for their visual impact, even the inedible ones. Not only are the colors fantastic, but the textures and light-manipulating properties of mushrooms never fail to amaze. The most translucent mushrooms are the *Hygrophori* and their allies, among which are found forms which seem to gather light in the darkest corners of the forest and beam it back with the effect of being lit from within. Their colors are reds, oranges and yellows, often all on the same mushroom.

There are some mushrooms whose surface textures suggest exotic materials—frosted glass, alien metallic alloys, wood or cloth or ancient paper, even the skin of animals. One section of the *Cortinarii* or web-veiled mushrooms contains metallic-skinned species of strange muted colors. Among mosses in the Catskill mountains we found silver *Cortinarii* along with the more conventional purple and lavender forms, that we could not find described in any mushroom guide. Most guides show only a dozen or so of the over 900 species of *Cortinarius* in North America. The amateur mushroomer has so little hope of making an exact identification of a mushroom in such a very large group. But it is also possible for anyone to find a species new to the science of mycology. If you have the ambition, it's a good idea to send specimens you can't identify to an expert mycologist. Mushrooms may be dried in a drying oven such as the ones used for drying fruit. They will keep for years and may be of scientific value if accompanied by detailed field data.

The fortuitous nature of mushroom identification from common published sources is illustrated by an experience we had in the summer of 1986 with a very strange mushroom we found in a woods we'd walked a few days before with a group of mushroom enthusiasts. As sometimes happens we found something we'd never seen before. On a woodland path through a grove of white pines and hemlocks we found a group of odd greenish mushrooms. They looked like some old crochet balls left in the woods to gather a matted coating of algae. Were these merely old mushrooms that had been here so long that algae grew on their caps? Only a woody fungus could last so long. When picked, these mushrooms proved quite fresh, and the sticky latex that exuded from the broken gills proved them to be *Lactarius.*

Meadow beauty (*Rhexia virginica*)

144

But after looking through all our mushroom books (and we have just about every general work on fungi published) we drew a blank. This must be a rare mushroom or even a new species, we thought. But answers are sometimes found in the most unlikely places. A few days later, after filing away the description of our peculiar *Lactarius*, we found a picture of it—in a coloring book! Later, in a monograph on *Lactarius* borrowed from a friend, we found an entry on *Lactarius atroviridis*, the black-green lactarius or milk-mushroom, and it was most definitely the one we'd found. Or was it? Professional mycologists have separated species of mushrooms on the basis of invisible characters—the structure of the microscopic spores or different responses of the spores or tissues to chemical reagents. Consequently, two mushrooms identical in appearance may not be the same species! I know of no other group of organisms with such difficult and perplexing systematics.

Despite the state of flux in mushroom systematics today, for centuries people have gathered mushrooms for food, usually relying on crude and inaccurate methods of distinguishing poisonous from non-poisonous types. Despite the availability of field guides written by professional mycologists, people are still sometimes poisoned by eating wild mushrooms. Surprisingly, it's sometimes the seasoned collectors who, in a moment of overconfidence, make a fatal misidentification.

There are a few mushrooms so distinct in appearance that anyone can learn quickly to recognize them with accuracy. Among edibles are the so-called "foolproof four"—the morels, the shaggy mane, the sulfur shelf and the oyster mushroom. The tooth fungi with their undersurface of hanging teeth are also very distinctive. Boleti are recognizable but the group contains a few poisonous species. These either have red undersides or stain blue when bruised, but not all red-bottomed or blue-stained boleti are poisonous. Better to skip some edibles than to take a risk on a poisonous one.

Boleti in general are distinguished from other groups of mushrooms by having a central stipe (stem) and pores rather than gills under the cap, but there is one species placed in the Boletacae that doesn't fit the mold, the paradoxically but accurately named gilled bolete. Another group of

Frondlet of marginal wood fern (*Dryopterus marginalis*)

Hygrophorus coccineus mushroom

False coral mushroom (*Tremellodendron pallidum*)

mushrooms, which includes the highly edible sulfur shelf or chicken mushroom, has pores but not (typically) a central stipe. These polypores, as they are called, are mostly tree parasites having the form of shelves.

Among gilled mushrooms, some groups are fairly easy to recognize. The milk mushrooms (genus *Lactarius*) exude a milky latex when broken. Their close relatives, the *Russulas*, are the most brittle of mushrooms; they crumble when their gills are rubbed.

Always to be avoided are specimens which fall into the murky category of "little brown mushrooms" (LBMs). There are hundreds of these look-alikes and a few of them are deadly. Mushroom poisoning takes several forms, not all of them fatal or even unpleasant. The effects range from simple stomach upset to nervous convulsions to blindness to hallucinations. The deadlier *Amanitas*—destroying angels and death caps— produce a sequence of symptoms including nausea, vomiting, convulsions, fever and chills about six to ten hours after consuming them. After several hours of these symptoms, the victim begins to "recover." But the sense of relief that comes with this false recovery is short-lived; in another day or half-day, the symptoms erupt again, this time leading almost invariably to death. Considering this, some may wonder why anyone dares to eat wild mushrooms of any sort. In fact, since the identification of mushrooms is so difficult and a mistake could be deadly, the nonexpert should not take the risk of eating what he or she finds.

The mushroom season continues well into autumn, when colorful mushrooms peek shyly from beneath fallen leaves of yellow and scarlet. Even in early winter, a few mushrooms may be found in a fresh state, including the edible velvet-foot, *Flammulina velutipes*.

Nature-lovers attracted to the minuscule or the bizarre may wish to become acquainted with the slime molds, organisms often grouped with the fungi, but significantly different in their way of life. Slime molds lead double lives, and the two life stages are so different as to be unrecognizable as the same organism.

At one stage, a slime mold lives up to its name, as a slithery blob of frothy ooze which moves at an imperceptible pace across the ground or

Swamp milkweed (*Asclepias incarnata*) seed pods.

over a log. This mass consists of countless amoeboid cells which feed on detritus, divide and multiply. This slimy stage appears in wet weather. Drying up usually triggers phase two, the stationary reproductive phase. Like fungi, slime molds produce spores from fruiting bodies, which in many cases resemble tiny mushrooms.

Until recently there was no source of information on slime molds short of esoteric scientific journals. Happily for those whose tastes run to the sublimely slimy, I can now refer the curious to Peter Katsaros' *Illustrated Guide to Common Slime Molds* (1989, Mad River Press, Eureka, CA). This field guide describes and illustrates with color plates 64 species of slime molds likely to be encountered in northeast forests.

The transition from late summer to autumn is marked by the onset of the color season, as trees stop photosynthesizing and transpiring water through their leaves. Other plants simply continue their cycles, providing no particular seasonal benchmarks. Some flowering herbs and grasses begin to set seed or die off, but others are just coming into bloom or have yet to bloom. The notion of autumn is more ours than Nature's.

Grape (*Vitis*) tendrils.

AUTUMN

AUTUMN is conveniently divided into two parts: the first, the color season of fall foliage; the second, the still mild period just before winter after the leaves are down, popularly called (if it's warm enough) Indian summer. This division is entirely natural, especially because the leaves of deciduous trees typically fall off in a relatively short period of time; in most parts of the Northeast sometime in October, in September in the northernmost parts of the region and in high mountains.

The change in leaves from green to other colors—yellows, oranges, reds, maroon, purples and browns—caused by the deterioration of chlorophyll, is autumn's most visible benchmark. This process is usually rather sudden and rapid, and often timed so as to coincide closely with the onset of frosty nights. But it is not frost, as is popularly believed, that causes the leaves to change colors; it is the abandonment of the leaves by the tree, which begins to withdraw its sap reserves into the lower trunk and rootstock. The attachment of leaf to twig is sealed off to conserve moisture. No longer engaged in the life processes of the tree, the leaves begin to die. The green pigment, chlorophyll, decays first, revealing more stable pigments of other colors. Eventually these too decay, leaving the drab brown leaves that cover the ground in late fall. Some hardwoods, especially oaks, retain some or nearly all of their leaves.

Temperature also does little to trigger the onset of leaf coloring. In any particular location, the trees (of a given species; different species turn color at different times) begin to turn color at almost the same time year after year, whether the weather is frosty or warm. Either an internal timing mechanism or a sensitivity to the shortening period of daylight as winter approaches makes trees start to winterize. Further south, deciduous trees shed their leaves in late autumn, even where the winters are mild and freezing spells are unusual.

Freezing weather can kill leaves before they change color. I have observed this in high mountains, where hard frosts may sometimes strike unexpectedly early, in August or early September. At this time, the trees' genetically-determined color-trigger has not yet gone off. There is probably too much cross-pollination between trees over a wide elevational

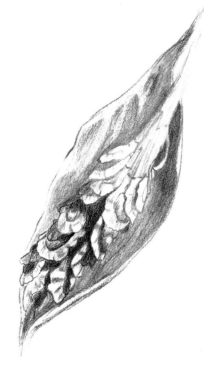

Common milkweed (*Asclepias syriaca*)

Previous pages:
Grassy Hill, Saugerties, New York

152

range to isolate genes which produce an earlier coloring of leaves in trees at the highest elevations.

Moisture can affect the color season in a number of ways. In a drought year, colors are not as vivid because there is simply not as much pigment in the leaves, and what there is fades faster. Hard rain may knock the weakly-connected colored leaves off the trees, leaving mostly green ones. Depending on the time of the season this happens, after a rain the forest may look either more summery than before or more wintry, but the ground will be quite colorful.

For brilliant fall foliage, adequate moisture from summer is more important than fall moisture, which often comes too late to make any difference. If autumn rains are light and not attended by high winds, leaves will stay on the trees. Frost has little effect except to make the leaves more picturesque by rimming them with ice crystals. Less damage to leaves by forest insects keeps leaves whole and attractive and also reduces the moisture loss that occurs with damaged leaves. An exception to this is the effect of gypsy moth larvae on oak leaves. When the caterpillars defoliate oaks in June, the leaves grow back in July. In the fall these leaves become vivid red, as they contain more tannins than spring leaves, a response both to the gypsy moth attack and to growing in hot, dry conditions. Undoubtedly there are many other factors, many probably unknown, which affect the color intensity of autumn leaves.

Once I stood with noted Catskill botanist Sherret Chase, gazing at an autumn hillside, wondering whether we could recognize different trees from the color of their fall foliage. We agreed there were a few tulip trees and a lot of sugar maples; the other things we could only guess at. But trying to tell trees by their fall colors is an interesting challenge.

Take those sugar maples. Sugar maple is a species whose leaves range widely in color once they lose their chlorophyll green. Some sugar maple trees turn a pale yellow, others a golden yellow, still others pumpkin orange, and loveliest of all, some go deep scarlet. The tulip trees we saw across the field were a pure lemon yellow. Hickories turn a more golden yellow, poplars pale yellow and ash leaves range from yellow to deep

Turtlehead (*Chelone glabra*) seed pods

153

Fringed gentians (*Gentiana crinita*)

Nightshade (*Solanum dulcamara*) berries

maroon, often on the same tree or even on the same leaf! So there may be great variation in one species (or one plant) and only the subtlest difference in color between two different species' leaves. This can be confusing. Perhaps the prettiest autumn leaves are those of a woodland shrub, maple-leaved viburnum. This plant is easily mistaken for a small maple except in the fall when its leaves are a delicate lavender or pale purple-maroon.

The reds are, of course, the favorite colors of many fall foliage fans. Which trees produce the most vivid reds? Certainly tupelo is a strong contender for the title of reddest of all with its simple, ovate, glossy leathery crimson leaves. Red maple always gives a strong showing, though its leaves are not always red (some trees produce yellow leaves or leaves mottled red and yellow). Certain oaks such as scarlet oak and less often white and chestnut oaks may produce vivid red leaves. Sassafras leaves are occasionally brilliant scarlet, but more often orange or yellow.

Trees are not the only plants which produce colorful autumn foliage. Shrubs do too, as do many herbs. Some of the prettiest fall scenery is found not in forests, but in brushlands or shrub-dominant plant communities such as scrub-oak barrens. A friend once described the colors of the shrubbery of the Albany Pine Bush in October as looking like a bowl of Trix cereal—the orange and yellows of dwarf oaks and the pinks and reds of blueberries and huckleberries. Brushy oldfields are also quite handsome in autumn, the blue-green of red cedars perfectly complemented by the maroon of gray-stem dogwood, while the golds of goldenrods and the blues of asters dance around them.

In moist fields and at the edges of streams and marshes the foliage of herbs takes command of the scene. That common invader of our wetlands, purple loosestrife, turns crimson in autumn and looks especially bright amidst the golden yellow of giant reed foliage shimmering in the fall breeze. The breeze loosens the silvery sailing seeds of the reeds, which join airborne seeds of milkweeds, black swallow-wort, early goldenrods and many other plants to drift away on the wind.

Autumn is the time, not only of colored leaves, but also of seed ripening and release, and of the final flowers of the year. The last

Beardtongue (*Penstemon digitalis*) seed pods

flowering plants of the year bloom in early autumn and set seed toward the end of the season, some just before winter. In that last gasp of warmth often called Indian summer, if it happens at all, strange things happen—plants of the spring may have a rare late fall blooming.

As we noted in the last chapter, the goldenrods and asters dominate the late season bloom boom, with other plants such as sunflowers and Joe-Pye-weeds adding secondary splashes of color. The Joe-Pyes seed quickly, but the others continue putting out blossoms well into the fall. A few flowers wait until late autumn to bloom.

Where the taller weeds are not so numerous as to shade out lesser plants, gentians may bloom. Most have blue-violet flowers, but a few have blooms of other hues. The most common is the closed or bottle gentian, whose flowers never open. They are fertilized by big bumblebees which pry them open temporarily to reach the nectar. Fringed gentian, a less common species, is spectacular, found growing in moist alkaline clays. Each flower lasts only a day or two, but each plant may bear up to half a dozen flowers in succession, and plants vary in the time they begin to produce flowers. Because of these delaying tactics, any population of gentians may produce blooms over a period of four to six weeks starting in early September. Two other species of gentian occur in the Northeast: the

Entoloma mushrooms

Rickenella fibula mushrooms

Hygrophorus mushroom
Collybia butyracea mushrooms

violet agueweed and the greenish striped gentian of the southern part of the region.

It is not unusual in autumn to find flowers whose main season of blooming is spring. Among garden plants, forsythia commonly sets a few blooms in fall, especially if warm weather continues into the late season. The wild plants which bloom again in fall are those which even in spring produce many blossoms over a relatively long period. Lyre-leaved rock cress and other wild mustards may do this, though some mustards such as toothworts never do. Herb-robert and harebell are often found in bloom well into autumn, but these are plants which bloom throughout the growing season if there is sufficient moisture. Often there is not, and they will go dormant during summer droughts. Perhaps rock cresses are no different, and their habit of dying back in summer is just the result of living in an extremely dry habitat. Cultivated spring-blooming plants such as four-o'clock and periwinkle also sometimes bloom in late fall.

Although some spring-blooming shrubs such as blueberries may bloom in fall, one forest shrub in the region habitually blooms in late autumn. Its thin-petalled yellow blossoms may not be noticed until the leaves have fallen from the trees and the colorful autumn foliage is no longer a distraction. At that time the flowers of the witch hazel become one of the prettiest sights in the bare woodlands of late autumn. Found throughout the Northeast in mixed hardwood forests, witch hazel does not occur in northern conifer forests. A related spring-blooming species, almost indistinguishable in appearance from native witch hazel, is sometimes planted as an ornamental.

Overall, few plants bloom in autumn; most are setting seed or have already done so in the summer. Autumn is harvest time in nature as well as on farms. The seeds of fall come in great variety. Many are too tiny to be noticed by creatures as large as people, but small creatures—little birds, mice and insects—seek them ravenously as they prepare for the long winter. The seeds which most attract us, and among wild seeds, those we make the most use of, are nuts and grains. Few people gather wild grain (grass seed) any more, but the kind most harvested, a staple of some groups of Native Americans, is wild rice, a wetland grass. Wild rice

Smooth false foxglove (*Gerardia flava*) seed pods

160

is still gathered for commercial sale and is very expensive. Few places in the Northeast provide enough of this grain to make gathering it worthwhile; it is most common in the wet prairie country of Wisconsin and Minnesota, but it occurs in eastern marshes.

Nuts, on the other hand, are abundant in the Northeast, most particularly acorns, the nuts of oaks. Though the native peoples used acorns for flour, and Europeans never adopted them for their culinary purposes, they are a staple of many animals' diets. Mice, chipmunks, squirrels, birds (especially blue jays) and many kinds of insects eat acorns. In fact, most acorns get eaten by something; few sprout to make seedlings, and even fewer of these seedlings grow into trees.

Like the woolly bear caterpillar, the acorn figures in a popular myth about predicting the severity of the coming winter. Abundant acorns or a great deal of acorn-harvesting activity among animals is widely believed to foretell a bad winter, the idea being that the animals somehow know the winter will be severe and so are gathering more stores than usual in preparation for the worst. In truth, it is the abundance of acorns which gets the animals excited and working so hard. Squirrels and chipmunks will always store as much food as they can; when acorns are abundant they go for acorns.

But why are acorns so incredibly numerous one year and scarce as hen's teeth the next? It seems that oaks are cyclic in their seed output; some populations in fact produce big acorn crops precisely every two years. This pattern prevails even in some mixed species populations. In a young oak woods in 1985, a year of acorn superabundance, white, chestnut, red and scarlet oaks all produced huge crops, while black and scrub oaks produced very few acorns. There are about a dozen species of oak in the Northeast (the southern "Hudson Valley" or "Carolinian" forests contain the greatest variety), so in any year there are probably good acorn crops in at least some places. No doubt many things affect acorn output—fertilization of oak flowers in spring, the summer moisture supply, insect attacks, etc. Acorns may also be aborted in their growth, as evidenced by dwarfed acorns in autumn, often quite dead and dried, abandoned by the tree earlier in the season under some unknown stress.

American hazelnuts/wild filberts (*Corylus americanus*)

161

Red maple (*Acer rubra*) leaf
Autumn leaves on the ground, Saugerties, New York

Bracken (*Pteridium aquilinum*)

Nuts more palatable to human taste are hickories and walnuts. Hickories are common trees in many types of forest. Shagbark hickory is the most widespread, both in terms of range and environmental conditions, found farther north (southern Maine) than any other hickory and common in forests of high and low moisture. It is often found with oaks and hop-hornbeam in dry uplands and with red maple, white ash, basswood and sycamore in floodplain forests. Its nuts are thick-shelled and meager of flesh. The best hickory nuts are those of the wild pecan of the southern states; all the northern nuts tend to be hard to crack and short on meat.

The walnuts are more worth seeking, though they are not as easy to deal with as "English" walnuts (actually, California walnuts). There are two species, butternut or white walnut and black walnut. The latter is now rare, having been overharvested for its extremely valuable lumber. Butternut is infrequent, but widely distributed. The nuts of black walnut are meaty, and though they are thick-shelled, they're delicious. Early settlers made a dye from the fibrous pulp that surrounds the inner nutshell. Butternuts are good, too, but thinner than black walnuts.

Today there are few black walnuts in the wild. Most trees are on farmlands or on country estates where they are loved and protected. In a

Collybia mushrooms

164

few places they have begun to repopulate nearby wild lands from these sanctuaries. This is a tree that could use some legal protection; individual large trees command prices of thousands of dollars as lumber, a great temptation to landowners. I have even found proof of walnut "poachers" on public lands.

Butternut is a more northern tree, an element of the northern hardwood forest community, but not a common one. This tree seems to do best in loose, rocky soil—talus, tailings or gravel. It is common enough in country that was quarried in the past, growing up in rubble after several decades of soil build-up. With sugar maple, white ash and basswood, it is also found in talus of deep mountain hollows.

The most attractive nuts of autumn are the wild hazelnuts. There are two species—American hazel of lowlands and beaked hazel of higher, cooler places. The nuts are almost identical to cultivated filberts, though usually a bit smaller. They are easy to extract and have an excellent flavor. Unfortunately, wild hazelnuts are not very common, and the nuts are seized almost immediately upon ripening by squirrels and chipmunks.

Berries form another large and familiar category of fruit. Though berries of many types appear from early summer onward, their production peaks in autumn. Even summer berries such as raspberries and blackberries may be found in September and October in the mountains, months after they've disappeared from the lower valleys. It is a common belief that most wild berries, except raspberries and blueberries, are poisonous. In fact, few are dangerous to eat, but most are unpleasantly bitter, astringent or tasteless.

Berries are a common element of decorative plant arrangements, especially holly and bittersweet berries. Evergreen hollies do not occur in the Northeast, but the common black or swamp holly (also called "winterberry") produces attractive berry arrangements, the numerous scarlet fruit tight against the black twigs. Bittersweet is a wild vine whose orange berries are at first contained within a shell, which as it ripens opens and folds back to surround the berries with the sections of the shell, like petals of a flower. These berries have the advantage of durability, while most other kinds tend to shrivel or rot, and fall off.

American bittersweet (*Celastrus scandens*) berry

Forked chickweed (*Paronychia fastigiata*)

Autumn woods in Saugerties, New York

Certain conspicuous fall fruits cannot be called nuts or berries or any other common name. What are we to call the little sticky globes that make up the red spires of staghorn sumac? The hollow pods of bladdernut are not really nuts, nor are the seeds inside nutlike. They are similar to the lantern-fruits of "japanese lantern" plants, which have a number of wild relatives with similar looking fruit, a papery shell containing one or more hard berries. These "ground cherries" attain a state of exquisite decay in late autumn when the fragile membrane is gone and only the lacy network of tougher veins remains.

Leaves, nuts, berries and other forms of fruit, and exotic objects such as insect galls and some kinds of cocoons all fall down in autumn. As animals seek out these varied plant and insect artifacts for food or shelter, the forest floor becomes a lively place.

The leaves of the forest hardwoods are the most numerous of autumn's ground detritus, and, as they accumulate, they hide many other things, including spiders and insects bedding down under the leaves for the winter and those actively hunting the others for food. Also under the leaves may be found mushrooms, which are able to fulfill their reproductive function without exposure to sunlight. Leaf-litter insects, slugs and snails eat the mushrooms, and aid in spreading their spores. Often humps of leaves tell of mushrooms directly beneath which have raised the leaves as they pushed upward in growth.

Fallen leaves are very important in conserving moisture for the trees and shrubs of the forest, and serve the same purpose for those herbs which live in dry forests, such as trailing arbutus. This protection is a trade-off with the more detrimental effect of the leaves' cutting off sunlight from ground plants. In early spring the leaves tend to break down rapidly or are blown away by the wind, allowing the herbaceous leaves access to sun.

By drifting and accumulating in some places while deserting others at the whim of the wind, the fallen leaves affect where plants will grow in spring. Many kinds of plants cannot seed into a bed of leaves, and will be absent from places where leaves accumulate.

Of course, autumn in a conifer forest is devoid of colored leaves except for those of the scattered birches and aspens which appear at intervals

Amanita mushroom

among the spruces and firs. One conifer of the north woods, the tamarack or American larch of northern wetlands, sheds its needles like a broad-leaved tree does its leaves. Pines also shed their needles in autumn. These needle-shedding conifers are quite capable of blanketing the ground with their discarded brown foliage, creating with the concentrated tannins in the needles a very acidic litter and contributing to the high acidity of northern forest soils. The litter of a conifer forest is by no means as lively as that of a hardwood forest, but it has its resident arthropods, and the seeds borne by cones attract red squirrels. Fall mushrooms bring out red-backed voles, plump northern woodland mice.

The farther north one goes the quicker the transition from summer to winter. Autumn on New York's Staten Island, in the zone of the Atlantic hardwood forest, is long and drawn out with a succession of tree species coloring and losing their leaves from late September through November. Long falls are typical of the entire Atlantic coast due to the tempering influence of the nearby ocean, but the fall begins progressively later as one travels from north to south. Inland and northward, autumns become brief and are sometimes cut short by winter conditions, as happens frequently in the Adirondacks of New York State and in other mountainous areas of the region.

Coral mushroom (*Ramaria*)

169

Harebell (*Campanula rotundifolia*)
Wintergreen (*Gaultheria procumbens*) berry

Seeds and pod of common milkweed (*Asclepias syriaca*)

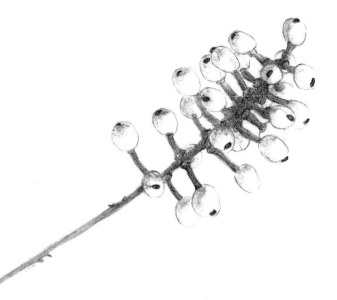

Even on a local scale, considerable variation may exist as to when signs of autumn first appear and how long they endure. Red maples in wetlands typically go red or yellow in advance of those rooted in moderately moist soil. By contrast, lakes and ponds typically exert a delaying of leaf fall upon the trees and shrubs on their shores. Trees in hollows protected from strong winds keep their leaves longer than those on exposed ridges.

Toward the close of autumn, frost becomes more and more frequent until almost as a rule the temperature dips below freezing at night. Plants vary greatly in their ability to remain unharmed by freezing temperatures; some wilt as soon as the air falls a little below freezing, while others can endure sub-zero temperatures with no ill effects whatsoever.

The first hard frost of the season leaves its mark upon the most fragile plants. People who garden known the fragility of tomatoes and squash which appear limp, wet and darkened after being frosted. Wild plants such as clearweed and white snakeroot are affected by the frost in the same way. There's nothing in nature more pathetic than a stand of jewelweed killed by the first frost, looking almost as if it had melted in the night, appearing more heatstruck than frostbitten.

By contrast, the raspberries and their relatives are amazingly hardy.

White baneberries/"doll's eyes"
(*Actaea pachypoda*)

172

They keep growing until the cold stops them, and yet these tenderest leaves are the ones which endure longest, staying green (or pinkish) beneath the winter snow and not dying off until spring revives the plant, at which time it begins to grow new leaves, giving little food and water to the extremities of the stems.

Mosses and lichens, our smallest plants, live almost in a world of their own, occupying territory only marginally habitable for other kinds of plants—rocks, old logs, dense nutrient-poor clays, peatlands (one type as we've seen is built by moss), tree trunks. These little plants thrive in the late autumn when temperatures fluctuate above and below freezing, with relatively little moisture loss. These plants can tolerate a daily cycle of freezing and thawing year-round, a situation mosses and lichens encounter in high mountains of the tropics, but not in temperate regions. In some habitats, they are the only green plants. Late autumn is the time they most often grow and reproduce. Mosses and lichens are the dominant plants in very high, windswept mountain peaks and on the northern tundra where permafrost keeps deep-rooting plants from gaining a foothold.

The forms and colors of mosses and lichens, especially of the reproductive parts, are fanciful and often quite elegant. Moss spore cases are borne on long, thin stalks which usually rise above the green part of the plant, which may be cushionlike or resemble some type of vascular plant, usually an evergreen, as evidenced by the name "cedar-moss." The spore cases are often bright red or yellow, and unusual in form, suggesting vases and urns or smoking pipes. A troop of them may suggest an army of alien beings on the march. To enjoy mosses one must crouch very low, actually lie belly down upon the ground. It helps to have a magnifying glass. Gazing into such a miniature landscape, it's hard not to be enchanted and intrigued. Some go on to take up moss study, a challenging discipline but less difficult than the study of mushrooms.

By the end of autumn, it takes just a simple event, a snowfall of a few inches, to tip the world straight into winter. Without a snowfall, autumn fades indiscernibly into the coldest season, and our realization of its passing comes only as we must bundle up more and more against the invading cold that marks the end of nature's year in the Northeast.

Hygrophorus mushroom

173

WINTER

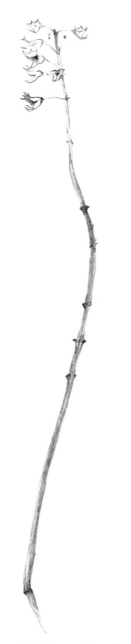

Papery bracts of skullcap (*Scutellaria*)

Previous pages:
View of Catskill Mountains from
Wittenberg Road, Woodstock, New York

WINTER'S sounds are raspy, brittle, desiccated. Walk through woods, brushland, or weedy meadow on a breezy day in early winter and you will hear the maracas, cymbals, and tambourines of the natural world. The fibrous husks of weeds, the stiffened leaves still clinging to twigs of oak, the hollow rattle of dry seed pods, enhance the lonely feeling of stark winter, like a die-hard percussion section deserted by all the melodic instruments of warmer seasons. Only the familiar babbling brook retains its sunny exuberance, and soon even its animated lilt will be muffled by a newly-formed layer of ice.

But the makers of the sound, they are but the toys of the wind, the life having left them with the passing of autumn. I like to follow those sounds to their various sources, to see which toy the wind is playing with, over beyond that ice-bedecked boulder or across the still unfrozen meadow stream. Often the loudest rattles emanate from a packet of seeds left by some plant for the wind to open and sow. It may be the brittle song of bladdernuts on slender twigs where these shrubs grow along some forested limestone ledge. Then again, it may be the soft rustle of seedbox stalks along a frozen stream or the whispering of dogbane pods and thistle heads in a brushy field.

What we see is skeletal, desiccated, deserted by the liquids of life and the colors of growth. Yet as the deer and rabbits know, beneath the snow lie leaves still green, the basal rosettes of perennials and the last growth of brambles whose ends lie close against the ground.

Winter is rightly regarded as the season of sleeping, when the plants and many of the animals of wild nature become inactive and wait out the cold weather. Some would judge winter dull, kindly allow it the benefit of being "quiet," or see only the harshness of winter that inconveniences people. All these things are true, but they give only a narrow understanding of winter and tell us nothing of the season's importance in the evolution of temperate organisms.

It would seem to be this annual period of cold, when water becomes bound up in a frozen state and remains unavailable as a mitigator of life processes, that has pressured organisms in temperate zones to evolve a seasonal life-style and all the remarkable adaptations that go with it. But cycles of wet and dry seasons also pressure plants and animals to evolve dormancy mechanisms and cycles; organisms tempered by wet/dry cycles may be pre-adapted to warm/cold cycles.

Winter always reminds me of the recent ice age when snow built up in the arctic year after year to form the slowly advancing ice mass. Some scientists believe the mild climate we are now enjoying is but an interlude between glacial advances. Perhaps the ice age is not really over. Our winters are yearly "little ice ages" and the ways in which organisms get through winter are the result of evolving through half a million years or more of ice age conditions.

Before the Pleistocene, the Earth's climate was milder even than now. Seasonal temperature differences in one area were not nearly as extreme as today's. But the climate had been cooling since the close of the Cretaceous some 60 million years before. This cooling trend favored organisms better adapted to cold, so when the glacial advances began about two million years ago, the stage was already set for the coming dominance of our present-day cold-hardy temperate zone organisms— among animals, the mammals and birds; among plants, deciduous trees and shrubs, and flowering plants. The ferns and conifers which survived the ice age are those best adapted to cold climates, and are in fact more abundant in northern and high-elevation floras.

Cold is the most obvious stress plants must endure in winter, but there are others, perhaps more important. Water loss is a great threat, especially because the dormant plants cannot take up water from their moorings in the soil, which for shallow-rooted herbs and shrubs may be frozen anyway. The measures by which plants conserve water in winter are varied and fascinating. Hardwoods drop their leaves, the biggest evaporating surfaces of the trees. Evergreens use different strategies: needles cut water loss by virtue of their greatly reduced surface areas and waxy coatings; leaves of evergreen broad-leaved shrubs such as rhododendrons and laurels curl up and point straight down in very cold weather, in effect making themselves more needle-like.

Winter temperatures go up and down randomly and vary more widely than growing season temperatures; one day the low may be near zero and

Thimbleweed (*Anemone virginiana*)

177

Pods of spreading dogbane (*Apocynum androsaemifolium*)

Japanese barberries (*Berberis thunbergii*)

a few days later the temperature goes up to fifty degrees. Winter warm spells could potentially "fool" organisms into spring activity, so temperate organisms have ways of sensing the difference between a winter warm spell and the real spring. Even a balmy January thaw won't con a tree into budding out, and January thaws can be very warm. I recall one at Ithaca, New York, when the temperature got into the seventies!

How do plants know that such a warm spell is not true spring? They use the same information people do to know what time it is, but their methods are different. We count days, compare them to celestial cycles, play with these numbers, and consequently set up our calendars. Plants may be unthawed and geared to sensitivity by warmth, but if the length of daylight is not correct for spring, they remain inactive. Only when the days are long enough—in March, April, May or even June, depending on latitude or elevation—do plants begin to bud and bloom or leaf out.

Some very small plants become intermittently active in winter, responding to warm spells by growing or engaging in reproductive activity. Primarily, these are the mosses and lichens, plants perhaps originally adapted to a rapidly oscillating frost-thaw cycle such as found on tropical mountaintops. In order to survive under those conditions, a plant must be able to turn itself on and off on short notice; it would have to evolve a quick response to warmth and cold. Small plants can do this precisely because they are small; a large plant needs more time to set itself up to grow or produce reproductive parts.

So the proverbial January thaw is a good time to examine mosses and lichens. In areas where trees predominate, lichens and mosses are found in greatest abundance and diversity on bedrock surfaces, poor, thin soils (particularly clays); and on the trees themselves, both living and dead. These little plants tolerate many small-scale stresses: the trampling of animal and human feet, natural forces of soil erosion, and the effects of freezing and thawing, which can disturb the structure of the soil and topple the tiny plants. Mosses and lichens survive these stresses by being rootless, or by carrying soil on their roots when they are uprooted, by being "modular"— that is, able to be broken up without being killed, and by a remarkable capacity to wait until conditions are more favorable again for growth.

Chicory (*Cichorium intybus*)

In the case of many lichens, their connection to a substrate is more for anchorage than for sustenance; they can be dislodged and kicked or blown about for months—perhaps for years—until they reach a hospitable shore, a rock or a tree stump where they can gain a new foothold. Some lichens, such as rock tripes, cannot reattach themselves to rocks. Mosses, though they resemble vascular plants, do not have the equivalent of roots. Still, they can stand to be dislodged and, so long as moisture is replenished often enough, can wait—even upside-down—for several months to be knocked into a good position for latching onto the ground again.

Plants with no exposure to light—those with no structure remaining above ground in the winter—must rely on other methods for knowing when spring has come. As the ground thaws, ice becomes water, stimulating the roots of plants to take it up, along with minerals needed for the growth of new leaves. The dark trunks of trees, warmed by the strong spring sun, soak up heat, allowing sap to flow again. Anyone who's made maple syrup knows the sap runs strong on sunny days and stops on cold nights.

The skunk cabbage, often considered a sign of spring, is more accurately a late winter blooomer, the first flowering plant to appear in our woods, even before the spring equinox, sometimes before the month of March. Most remarkably, it literally burns its way through the decaying ice and snow of late February or March, a little furnace with a body temperature only about 25°F below that of a warm-blooded mammal.

In any population of skunk cabbage, there is tremendous variation among individuals in terms of the time of blooming. In one patch of wooded swamp I found skunk cabbages in fresh bloom over a period of two months. The later individuals may survive late extreme cold or encounter swarms of insect pollinators where the early bloomers did not.

It's a mystery how the skunk cabbage senses when to begin sending its burning bud up through the frozen ground. Perhaps a chemical "clock" marks off time, so that the plant is not dependent upon an external stimulus to trigger growth. Such chemical clocks are common enough in insects, especially in dormant stages such as eggs and pupae. Probably they occur in plants as well. This is not to say that environmental

Japanese barberries (*Berberis thunbergii*)

181

Fruit of multiflora rose (*Rosa multiflora*)

Reindeer lichen (*Cladina*)

conditions have no influence whatsoever. I once found a skunk cabbage colony growing below a bank near a housing development from which issued warm graywater effluent. In this spot, the plants bloomed prodigiously early, in mid-January. These effluent-influenced plants paid for their precociousness one year when a sub-zero February cold spell freezer-burned the plants' blossoms to black, shriveled husks. Other plants out of the way of the effluent bloomed later and were spared the frost.

The skunk cabbage is unique among our northern flora in its heat-generating ability. It is a tropical plant which has fought its way north, and probably the wide variation in blooming time among individuals has aided it in its northward push.

Even with plants' many adaptations to winter, the season's stresses do weaken and ultimately lead to the deaths of countless plants. Ice storms break off the twigs and branches of trees, later permitting entry of fungal spores and wood-boring insects. Extremely cold periods with no snow cover can lead to desiccation and freezing off of the basal leaves of small, ground-hugging herbs. With no leaves to gather sunlight in spring, the plants may die or perform too poorly that season to compete with stronger plants.

Winter's influence may thus change the make-up of a plant community, even in the course of only a few years. The result is that temperate plant communities are always in flux, always full of surprises for the nature-lover.

Though the entire Northeast has fairly cold winters, with some freezing even in the southernmost part of the region, the length and severity of winter varies widely. The season is longest and harshest in the north and in the higher elevations of any part of the region. This variation creates a greater variety of plant communities. For instance, in mountainous

Evening lychnis (*Lychnis alba*)

184

regions with long winters and short growing seasons, plants of the far north are found far south of their lowland ranges. The vegetation of mountains resembles that of the conifer forests and tundra of northern Canada where winters are similarly long and the growing season similarly short.

It is worth a walk in the higher reaches of one of the great mountain ranges of the New England or New York State to see just how awesome winter can be in these lofty heights.

Gazing up from valley level on a mid-winter morning, one sees on the mountain a horizon above which everything is a more brilliant white. This is the hoarfrost zone where moisture in the air condenses as frost directly on to the trees, shrubs, rocks and grasses. The frost builds up in this way during the fall and its weight upon the plants is later supplemented by the snows of winter. All this weight breaks many twigs and branches off trees in this zone, the more so because the twigs are rendered brittle by the tremendous cold.

On reaching the hoarfrost zone, the walker sees bizarre, sawtoothed fins of snow-ice on the branches of all the trees. The dead grasses sparkle with rims of rime. In the hollow of a tree is a perfect, ice-laced spider web, relic of the last fifty-degree day before the deep freeze set in to stay. And though the fragile web survived in its windless nook, at the edge of a great mountain cliff, the wind's work is impressively visible. Twisted trees face the open valley below with bare and broken fronts, while the backsides of such trees are the only parts with foliage, and this is most lush in a long trailing mat extending off behind the cliff along the ground.

A dead spruce with its bark long gone shows a twisted, spiraling grain, an adaptation of growth which adds strength to its structure, enabling it to withstand the gale-force winds of the open mountain ledges. Is it any wonder there are no human habitations on the Northeast's highest mountaintops?

The influence of cold-weather trends on the flora of northern regions is considerable; it is the master factor shaping the natural diversity and character of the plant communities of the Northeast.

Other plants become intermittently active in winter, responding quick-

Yucca (*Yucca filamentosa*)

185

ly to the very warm spells that other plants ignore, engaging in growth or reproduction. These plants are small and shallow-rooted, primarily mosses and lichens, the latter which are not really rooted at all, but merely attached to rocks and trees. Unlike trees and shrubs, these plants can take up moisture during winter thaws by tapping the thin layer of surface soil from which the ice has temporarily given way to water.

This capacity of mosses and lichens to turn on and off rapidly in response to thawing and freezing allows them to survive in mountainous districts with a daily freeze-thaw cycle. In the highest elevations of the Northeast, occasional night temperatures even during the summer may reach or fall below the freezing point. Here, as nowhere else, the mosses and lichens hold sway, dominating the treeless landscape. These alpine gardens are much like the arctic tundra, but rockier and far more picturesque.

But mosses and lichens are found in all habitats of the region. Just look in the deep, moist woodlands under the pines and hemlocks and on their great trunks. The rock ledges of river banks and mountain slopes abound in these tiny plants, and they afford a point of living interest for the winter walker. You must crouch low, even lie upon the ground to take them in. With their conifer-like stalks and leaves and their alien-looking long-stalked spore-cases, mosses create a micro-world of inexhaustible fascination.

Mosses and lichens, particularly the latter, can to a great extent survive being dislodged and blown about by erosional forces or by the activities of animals (digging beasts like skunks and groundhogs, and scrapers such as deer and moose). A little piece of lichen, dislodged by a deer's hoof (or a hiker's boot) may blow away and, months later, find itself a hospitable place from which it eventually expands to form a new colony of its kind.

Vascular plants (those which, unlike mosses and lichens, have inner, fluid-transporting vessels), though dormant in winter, remain active in a way. Their dessicated remains are blown about over the snow and ice by winter winds. Thus are seeds cast far and wide, with soil-building detritus to nurture them when they sprout in spring.

Snowdrops (*Galanthus nivalis*)
Peter's Field, Woodstock, New York

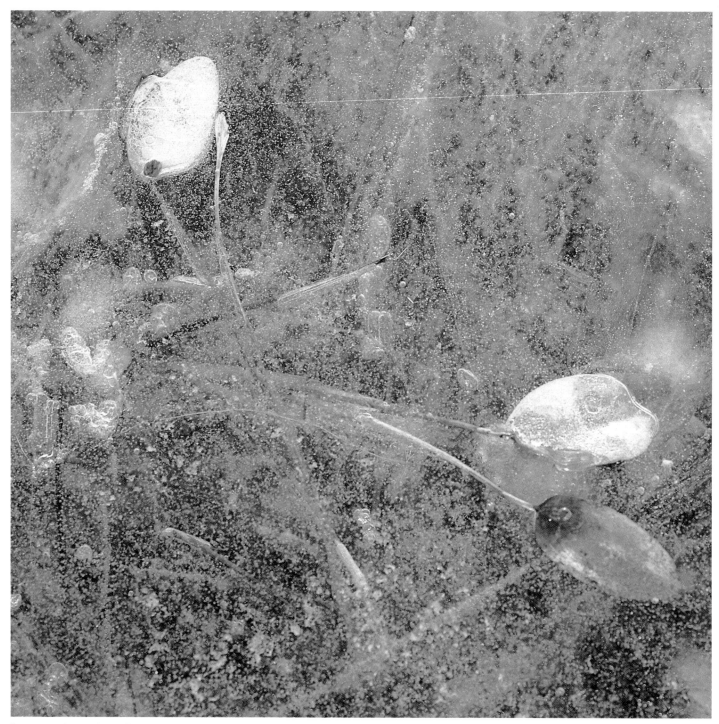

Leaves of pondweed (*Potamogeton natans*)

THOSE who live near one of the rarer, more remarkable environments of the Northeast are indeed lucky, though they may not know it. A trip to a bog, fen, tidal marsh, alpine meadow, pine or pavement barrens is always worthwhile. If you are not very familiar with your proximate surroundings, explorations close to home are almost bound to turn up a few small-scale examples of odd habitat. Mini-pavement barrens are scattered along the Hudson Valley near our home town of Saugerties, New York. I found a gorgeous shale barren in an urban area near Kingston, New York, a place with the largest colony of prickly pear cactus I've ever found along with lyre-leaved rock cress (typically a cliff plant), scrub oak (a pine-barrens element), and red cedar (an oldfield denizen). Such floral smorgasbords are always a pleasure to an appreciative nature walker.

The Kingston cactus flats are a reminder of how haphazard is our stewardship of natural diversity. That a patch of rare habitat remained relatively undisturbed (the place was host to beer-drinking teenagers who built campfires and littered) in a very densely developed township is one of those random miracles biologists are continually coming across. Unfortunately, the miracles don't last. The prickly pear is now gone and in its place stands a housing project. There are not enough informed naturalists prowling every acre of the Northeast to secure every square foot of unusual environmental real estate. Much has been lost and much will continue to be lost.

Still, there is hope. More than ever in the last three decades environmentalists have been exploring the region, finding rare habitats, and securing these places against the onslaught of developers. This task is not an easy one; the courts are not likely to decide in favor of preservation unless it is shown that endangered or threatened species are present and that the proposed development would destroy these species at that location. The Nature Conservancy acts by purchasing outright valuable natural lands, then adding them to its holdings or turning them over to state conservation agencies. The organization also seeks conservation easements in which the owner of a tract promises not to alter the habitat in exchange for tax abatement or other benefits.

Pennyroyal (*Hedeoma pulegioides*)

The conservation movement began as a grassroots effort, and it is important not to lose that common base, for it is the foundation of all conservation, even now that organizations such as the Nature Conservancy, the Natural Resources Defense Council, the Sierra Club and the Wilderness Society have given the movement a more corporate attitude and methodology. The truth is that as much as you may contribute to conservation groups, you can do more by becoming familiar with your own neighborhood, finding the most important natural habitats and unusual plant populations, and bringing these to the attention of local chapters of conservation groups or local boards of government which may be amenable to zoning such lands off limits to development. Most states in the region have natural heritage programs which use various legal procedures to preserve rare plants and animals and their habitats.

Anyone taking up this task must be sufficiently educated in plant and plant community recognition to know what's rare and unusual and what's simply pretty. The most unusual and important habitats are often perceived negatively by those unversed in the lore of rare environments. Pine and pavement barrens are often looked upon as ugly, stark places, hence the name "barrens." Bogs and marshes are usually hated for their mosquitoes and biting flies, not loved for their rare butterflies, salamanders and orchids.

Fortunately, there are many books with clear photographs or drawings of plants and their diagnostic characters. These field guides also contain brief descriptions of seasonal appearance and typical habitat, and the range and rarity of a plant. Also, by joining a local chapter of the Nature Conservancy, Sierra Club or a local natural history society, you will meet people who know plants and mushrooms and the most interesting natural sites in your area. The proximity of a university or natural history museum is another great boon to the budding naturalist, for there will be scientists familiar with the local environment and willing to direct any sincere amateur to places of natural interest and beauty.

The opportunity exists for the reclamation of lost habitat, and here a knowledge of soils and succession dynamics is indispensable. Sometimes rare plants can be re-established in places where they have been extinguished, once conditions there are stabilized. Or if a colony of some uncommon but not endangered plant is threatened by development, an informed amateur naturalist may learn how to transplant the plants to a place with the proper environmental conditions.

Rarities are the first concern of conservationists because they are in the most danger of being lost forever, but there is a second line of defense which has received little attention. The loss of commonplace wild habitat presents the prospect of uncommon species becoming rare in the future, and of common species eventually becoming uncommon. In addition, the expansion of species-poor artificial environments—residential areas with their lawns and cultivated shrubs and industrial parks and shopping centers with their tiny islands of wood chips and planted trees—has made natural environments less and less a part of everyday experience.

The encouragement of the use of native plants in landscaping projects is an important part of the modern conservationist's modus operandi. Some landscaping firms in the Northeast are now working primarily with native species. The inclusion of native plants in seed and garden catalogs and the increasing popularity of "butterfly gardening" (planting species which are nectar sources or larval hosts of native butterflies) are helping to make some residential grounds into wild sanctuaries rather than lawn zones from which these weeds are forcibly excluded. Letting part of the lawn go back to nature saves work as well as wild plants.

Although the subject of animals is not central to this book, it is important to remember that in securing plant communities, refuges for animals are also created. These refuges are especially important to insects, birds, small mammals, reptiles and amphibians—all small creatures with small home ranges and special habitat requirements.

The more patches of wild plant communities we secure, the more these island wildernesses will serve to prove to people, with their beauty and natural diversity, that preservation is worth the effort. In a way, those refuges closest to human population centers are the most important, because there, the greatest number of people will come to know them. Familiarity with such places and their resident organisms, far from breeding contempt, more often fosters a caring interest and enduring love.

Crabapples (*Malus*) with raindrops

BIBLIOGRAPHY

Arora, David. *Mushrooms Demystified*. Berkeley, CA: Ten Speed Press, 1986.

Atwood, Stanley Bearce. *The Length and Breadth of Maine*. Maine Studies #96; Orono, ME: University of Maine Press, 1973.

Brooks, Karl L. *A Catskill Flora and Economic Botany*. Albany, NY: New York State Museum, State Education Department, 1979 (in progress).

Brown, Lauren. *Weeds in Winter*. New York; W.W. Norton & Company, Inc., 1976.

Cobb, Boughton. *A Field Guide to Ferns and Their Allies*. Boston: Houghton Mifflin, 1956.

Conrad, Henry S., and Paul L. Redfearn, Jr. *How to Know the Gilled Mushrooms*. Dubuque, IA: William C. Brown, 1979.

Cox, Barry C. *Biogeography: An Ecological and Environmental Approach*. New York: Wiley, 1980.

Forman, Richard T. T. *Fine Barrens, Ecosystem and Landscape*. New York: New York Academic Press, 1979.

Glasser, John W. H. *A Naturalist's Handbook to the White Mountains*. Boston: Appalachian Mountain Club, 1977.

Harlow, William M. *Trees of the Eastern and Central United States and Canada*. New York: Dover Publications, 1963.

Harris, Stuart K.; Jean H. Langenheim; Frederick L. Steele; and Miriam Underhill. *Field Guide to Mountain Flowers of New England*. Boston: Appalachian Mountain Club, 1977.

Hale, Mason E. *How to Know the Lichens*. Dubuque, IA: William C. Brown, 1979.

Henley, Thomas A., and Sweet, Neesa *Hiking Trails in the Northeast*. Matteson, IL: Great Lakes Living Press, 1976.

Hitchcock, A. S. *Manual of the Grasses of the United States*. New York: Dover Publications, 1971.

Hitchcock, Charles Henry. *Geology of New Hampshire: A Report*. Concord, NH: New Hampshire State Geologist, 1978.

Hotchkiss, Neil. *Common Marsh Plants of the United States and Canada*. New York: Dover Publications, 1972.

Katsaros, Peter. *Illustrated Guide to Common Slime Molds*. Berkeley, CA: Mad River Press, 1989.

———. *Familiar Mushrooms of North America*. New York: Alfred A. Knopf, 1990.

Klaber, Doretta. *Violets of the United States*. Cranbury, NJ: A. S. Barnes, 1976.

Kilcher, John C., and Morrison, Gordon. *A Field Guide to Eastern Forests*. Boston: Houghton Mifflin, 1964.

Krieger, Louis C. C. *The Mushroom Handbook*. New York: Dover Publications, 1967.

Kudish, Michael. *Paul Smiths Flora*. vols. 1 and 2. Paul Smiths, NY: Paul Smiths College, 1975, 1981.

Johnson, Charles W. *Bogs of the Northeast*. Hanover, NH, and London: University Press of New England, 1985.

Lange, Jacob E.; Morton Lange; and F. B. Hora. *Mushrooms and Toadstools*. New York: E. P. Dutton, 1963.

Larsen, James Arthur. *Ecology of the Northern Lowland Bogs and Conifer Forests*. New York: Academic Press, 1982.

Lincoff, Gary H. *The Audubon Society Field Guide to North American Mushrooms*. New York: Alfred A. Knopf, 1981.

Little, Elba L. *The Audubon Society Field Guide to North American Trees*. New York: Alfred A. Knopf, 1980.

McCormick, Jack. *The Pine Barrens: Vegetational Geography*. Trenton: New Jersey State Museum, 1973.

McIlvaine, Charles, and Robert K. MacAdam. *One Thousand American Fungi*. New York: Dover Publications, 1973.

McKnight, Kent H., and Vera E. *A Field Guide to Mushrooms of North America*. Boston: Houghton Mifflin, 1987.

McMartin, Barbara. *Discover the Eastern Adirondacks*. Woodstock, VT: Backcountry Publications, 1988.

———. *Discover the Southern Adirondacks*. Woodstock, VT: Backcountry Publications, 1988.

Miller, Oren K. *Mushrooms of North America*. New York: E. P. Dutton, 1985.

Mitchell, Richard S., and Charles T. Sheviak. *Rare Plants of New York State*. Albany: New York State Museum, State Education Department, 1981.

Newcombe, Lawrence. *Newcombe's Wildflower Guide*. Boston and Toronto: Little, Brown, 1977.

Niering, William A. *The Audubon Society Field Guide to North American Wildflowers*. New York: Alfred A. Knopf, 1979.

Pacioni, Giovanni (Lincoff, U.S. ed.), *Simon and Schuster's Guide to Mushrooms*. New York: Simon and Schuster, 1981.

Peterson, Roger Tory, and Margaret McKenny. *A Field Guide to Wildflowers of North America*. Boston: Houghton Mifflin, 1968.

Petrides, George A. *A Field Guide to Trees and Shrubs*. Boston: Houghton Mifflin, 1964.

Pielom, E. C. *Biogeography*. New York: Wiley, 1979.

Rittner, Donald, ed., et al. *Pine Bush: Albany's Last Frontier*. Albany: Pine Bush Historic Preservation Project, 1976.

Rupp, Rebecca. *Red Oaks and Black Birches*. Powval, VT: Garden Way Press, 1990.

Seymour, Frank Conkling. *The Flora of New England*. Rutland, VT: Charles E. Tuttle, 1969.

Shelford, Victor. *The Ecology of North America*. Urbana, IL; Chicago; London: University of Illinois Press, 1978.

Smith, Alexander H.; Helen V. Smith; and Nancy S. Weber. *How to Know the Gilled Mushrooms*. Dubuque, IA: William C. Brown, 1981.

———. *How to Know the Non-gilled Mushrooms*. Dubuque, IA: William C. Brown, 1981.

Symonds, George W. D. *The Shrub Identification Book*. New York: William Morrow, 1963.

———. *The Tree Identification Book*. New York: William Morrow, 1963.

Tiner, Ralph W. *A Field Guide to Coastal Wetland Plants of the Northeastern United States*. Amherst: University of Massachusetts Press, 1987.

Venning, Frank D. *A Guide to Field Identification of Wildflowers of North America*. New York: Golden Press, 1984.

Wiley, Farida A. *Ferns of Northeastern United States*. New York: Dover Publications, 1964.

GENERAL INDEX

195

Mycelium (pl., mycelia), 133, 136
Mycologist, expert, 144–45
Mycophage (mushroom eater), 141
Mycophile (mushroom lover), 136; arthropods, 141
Mycorrhizal fungi, 133, 136, 140

Native Americans, 23, slash-and-burn farming, 33; used acorns, 161
Natural Heritage Programs, 190; New York, rare plant list, 124
Natural Resources Defense Council, 190
Nature Conservancy, 189–90
Nature, curiosity about, 9
Nature preserves, guide to, 16
Needles, pine, shed in autumn, 169
New England: coastal lowland, 61; grasslands, 36
New Jersey, dwarf pine barrens, 29
New York counties: Greene, 40; Jefferson, 48; Ulster, 40
New York municipalities: Albany, 10, 32, 156; Ithaca, 180; Kingston, 189; New York City, 37; Rosendale, 43; Sawkill, **22;** Saugerties, **166,** 189; Staten Island, 169; Troy, 37; Woodstock, **174-75, 187**
New York State, 21, 29, 40, 125
Northeastern United States, 16–17, 24
Nuts, 160–61, 164–65; acorns, 160; hazelnuts, 165; hickory, 164; walnuts, 164–65

Oldfields: in autumn, 156; development, 36; from hayfields or cow pastures, 49
Onondaga Lake, 128
Ontario Lake Plain, 28, 37, 40, 61, 92
Outwash plains, 60, 64, 141

Parasitic fungus, alien on American chestnut, 137
Peat, 32, 40–41
Peatlands, 173
Peck, Charles H. (mycologist), 133
Penicillin, 136
Permafrost, 173
Photoperiod, 57, 152, 180
Photosynthesis, 81, 109, 149
Piedmont, 23
Pigments, 152
Plant communities, 7, 17, 24, 120; beaches, 104; mountain compared with lowland, 48; saving, 191
Plants: adaptation to grazing, 89; aquatic, 96; arctic/alpine, 105, 108; attract insects, 93; avoid competition, 93; carnivorous, 96–97; collecting, 120; creeping, 92, 97; dependent on fungi, 136; dryland, 101, 103; dwarf,

105; identifying mystery, 121–22; as indicators of soil and climate, 20; landscaping with native, 191; not fooled into thinking it's spring, 180; parasitic, 129; propagation by runners, 89; rare, 45, 105, 108, 190, 191; recognizing before they bloom, 61; return from the dead, 124–25; resistant to mowing and herbicides, 124; roadside, 120; second blooming in fall, 129; single-species stands, 129; small, 85, 88, 117, 180; that signal summer, 88; tall, 88, 101; western, in Northeast, 24; wetland, 93, 96–97, 100. winter stress, 184; *See also:* Alien plants; Forests; Herbs; Trees; Wetlands; Wildflowers *and separate Plant Index*
Pleistocene epoch, 20, 29, 177
Poachers, walnut, 165
Point Pelee, Ontario, TV documentary, 9
Poisonous mushrooms, 137, 140, 145, 148
Pollen from bogs, 23, 41
Pollination, 58, 89
Ponds, 36, 44, 56
Pores of mushrooms, 137, 145, 148
Prairies, counterparts to western, 36
Predators on insects, 128
Predictions, severity of winter, 161
Progression of fall, 169, 172, 173

Quarries, arbutus in, 60
Quebec, 25, 125

Rabbits, 176
Rain: effect on color change, 153; washing bedrock, 44
Rain forests, 41
Recognizing plants at any time of year, 81
Red: as a color found in many bog plants, 97; as a favorite fall color, 156
Repeat visits to same site, 77, 97
Rhododendron hells, 112
Rice, wild, 160–61
Rivers, Joan, Show, 9
Rocks: crevices sheltering plants, 45; ridges on mountains, 80; moss and lichen on, 45, 173
Rotters, 133
Runners, plant propagation by, 89

Sand, 23, 29
Sandplains, 101, 103, 113
Sandstone, 69
Sap, 53, 181
Sedges: alpine, 108; in wet/dry areas, 100
Seed capsules to identify violets, 73
Seed dispersal, 156–57

Seed pods; earlier development at mountain base, 72
Seed race, 57
Seeds: alien, 24; blown about by winter winds, 186; end of summer, 149; in fall, 160; after the ice age, 29; in midsummer, 116, 117; pine cone, 169; in spring, 78, 81; tree, 53; washed onto floodplains, 28; in winter, 176
Sequence of blooming, 53
Shale, 69
Shrubs of conifer forests, 25; of mountains, 76–77, 113; of northern hardwood forest, 26; oak in pine barrens, 29; in oldfields, 48; in poor soil, 45; root in rocks, 68; spring-blooming in fall, 160; in sunny openings, 26; in swamps, 32
Sierra Club, 190
Skunk cabbage as heating plant, 58
Skunks, 186
Slabrock, 44
Slime molds, 148/–49
Slugs, 168
Snails, 168
Snakes, hognose on TV, 9
Snow, 56, 76, 173; covering still-green leaves, 176; skunk cabbage melts, 58
Soil: accumulating in rocks, 65, 68; in bogs, 23, 41; clay with lichen and moss, 173, 180; clay in wet/dry areas, 100; disturbed, as places for alien plants, 24; in former pastures, 49; on glaciers, 21; infused with mycelia, 136; lichen powder and rock particles, 45; loose rocky with butternut, 165; morels on limey, 78; mountain slope, 72, 73; in pine barrens, 29; poisoning by plants (sunflowers), 129; poor, 92; preferred by skunk cabbage, 58; of rock ridges, 80; thawing, 53, 84–85; wetland, 33, 40
Solstice, 81, 116
Spiders: bedding down or hunting, 168; web, **38,** 185
Spring, timing of, 52, 81
Spring flowers blooming in autumn, 157, 160
Squirrels, 161, 165; red, 169
States (of U.S.): Georgia, 21; Maine, 25, 164; Minnesota, 161; New Jersey, 29, 104; New Hampshire, 25; Pennsylvania, 21, 45, 125; Rhode Island, 29; Vermont, 25; Wisconsin, 161. *See also:* New York State
Stipe (stem) of mushrooms, 141, 145, 148
Streams: cardinal flower in, 120; in early winter, 176; good for wildflowers in spring, 61; from mountain bedrock, 73; as openings in forest canopy, 109; Sawkill Creek, **22;** too fast for plants, 44

PLANT INDEX

198

28; on TV, 9
Tupelo, 28, 32, 137; in fall, 156
Walnut, 48, 164-65; black, 78, 164; English/
    California, 164; nuts, 164; white
    (butternut), 26, 73, 164-65
Willow, 28, 53; black, 28; weeping as alien,
    57; pussy, 28, 53; catkins, 77

INDEX OF LATIN NAMES